Bloom's BioCritiques

Dante Alighieri
Maya Angelou
Jane Austen
The Brontë Sisters
Lord Byron
Albert Camus
Geoffrey Chaucer
Anton Chekhov
Joseph Conrad
Stephen Crane
Charles Dickens
Emily Dickinson
William Faulkner
F. Scott Fitzgerald
Robert Frost
Ernest Hemingway
Langston Hughes
Stephen King
Arthur Miller
John Milton
Toni Morrison
Edgar Allan Poe
J. D. Salinger
William Shakespeare
John Steinbeck
Henry David Thoreau
Mark Twain
Alice Walker
Walt Whitman
Tennessee Williams

Bloom's BioCritiques

ALBERT CAMUS

Edited and with an introduction by
Harold Bloom
Sterling Professor of the Humanities
Yale University

CHELSEA HOUSE
PUBLISHERS
A Haights Cross Communications Company
Philadelphia

©2003 by Chelsea House Publishers, a subsidiary of
Haights Cross Communications.

A Haights Cross Communications Company

Introduction © 2003 by Harold Bloom.

Printed and bound in the United States of America.

10 9 8 7 6 5 4 3 2 1

Library of Congress Cataloging-in-Publication Data

Albert Camus / edited and with an introduction by Harold Bloom.
        p. cm. -- (Bloom's biocritiques)
Includes bibliographical references and index.
    ISBN 0-7910-7381-5
    1. Camus, Albert, 1913-1960--Criticism and interpretation. I. Bloom,
Harold. II. Series.
    PQ2605.A3734Z546113 2003

                                    2003000804

Chelsea House Publishers
1974 Sproul Road, Suite 400
Broomall, PA 19008-0914

http://www.chelseahouse.com

Contributing editor: Jenn McKee

Cover design by Keith Trego

Cover: © Bettmann/CORBIS

Layout by EJB Publishing Services

CONTENTS

User's Guide

These volumes are designed to introduce the reader to the life and work of the world's literary masters. Each volume begins with Harold Bloom's essay "The Work in the Writer" and a volume-specific introduction also written by Professor Bloom. Following these unique introductions is an engaging biography that discusses the major life events and important literary accomplishments of the author under consideration.

Furthermore, each volume includes an original critique that not only traces the themes, symbols, and ideas apparent in the author's works, but strives to put those works into a cultural and historical perspective. In addition to the original critique is a brief selection of significant critical essays previously published on the author and his or her works followed by a concise and informative chronology of the writer's life. Finally, each volume concludes with a bibliography of the writer's works, a list of additional readings, and an index of important themes and ideas.

HAROLD BLOOM

The Work in the Writer

Literary biography found its masterpiece in James Boswell's *Life of Samuel Johnson*. Boswell, when he treated Johnson's writings, implicitly commented upon Johnson as found in his work, even as in the great critic's life. Modern instances of literary biography, such as Richard Ellmann's lives of W. B. Yeats, James Joyce, and Oscar Wilde, essentially follow in Boswell's pattern.

That the writer somehow is in the work, we need not doubt, though with William Shakespeare, writer-of-writers, we almost always need to rely upon pure surmise. The exquisite rancidities of the Problem Plays or Dark Comedies seem to express an extraordinary estrangement of Shakespeare from himself. When we read or attend *Troilus and Cressida* and *Measure for Measure*, we may be startled by particular speeches of Ulysses in the first play, or of Vincentio in the second. These speeches, of Ulysses upon hierarchy or upon time, or of Duke Vincentio upon death, are too strong either for their contexts or for the characters of their speakers. The same phenomenon occurs with Parolles, the military impostor of *All's Well That Ends Well*. Utterly disgraced, he nevertheless affirms: "Simply the thing I am/Shall make me live."

In Shakespeare, more even than in his peers, Dante and Cervantes, meaning always starts itself again through excess or overflow. The strongest of Shakespeare's creatures—Falstaff, Hamlet, Iago, Lear, Cleopatra—have an exuberance that is fiercer than their plays can contain. If Ben Jonson was at all correct in his complaint that "Shakespeare wanted art," it could have been only in a sense that he may not have intended. Where do the personalities of Falstaff or Hamlet touch a limit? What was it in Shakespeare that made the two parts of *Henry IV* and *Hamlet* into "plays unlimited"? Neither Falstaff nor Hamlet will be stopped: their wit, their beautiful, laughing speech, their intensity of being—all these are virtually infinite.

In what ways do Falstaff and Hamlet manifest the writer in the work? Evidently, we can never know, or know enough to answer with any authority. But what would happen if we reversed the question, and asked: How did the work form the writer, Shakespeare?

Of Shakespeare's inwardness, his biography tells us nothing. And yet, to an astonishing extent, Shakespeare created our inwardness. At the least, we can speculate that Shakespeare so lived his life as to conceal the depths of his nature, particularly as he rather prematurely aged. We do not have Shakespeare on Shakespeare, as any good reader of the Sonnets comes to realize: they do not constitute a key that unlocks his heart. No sequence of sonnets could be less confessional or more powerfully detached from the poet's self.

The German poet and universal genius, Goethe, affords a superb contrast to Shakespeare. Of Goethe's life, we know more than everything; I wonder sometimes if we know as much about Napoleon or Freud or any other human being who ever has lived, as we know about Goethe. Everywhere, we can find Goethe in his work, so much so that Goethe seems to crowd the writing out, just as Byron and Oscar Wilde seem to usurp their own literary accomplishments. Goethe, cunning beyond measure, nevertheless invested a rival exuberance in his greatest works that could match his personal charisma. The sublime outrageousness of the Second Part of *Faust*, or of the greater lyric and meditative poems, form a Counter-Sublime to Goethe's own daemonic intensity.

Goethe was fascinated by the daemonic in himself; we can doubt that Shakespeare had any such interests. Evidently, Shakespeare abandoned his acting career just before he composed *Measure for Measure* and *Othello*. I surmise that the egregious interventions by Vincentio and Iago displace the actor's energies into a new kind of mischief-making, a fresh opening to a subtler playwriting-within-the-play.

But what had opened Shakespeare to this new awareness? The answer is the work in the writer, *Hamlet* in Shakespeare. One can go further: it was not so much the play, *Hamlet*, as the character Hamlet, who changed Shakespeare's art forever.

Hamlet's personality is so large and varied that it rivals Goethe's own. Ironically Goethe's Faust, his Hamlet, has no personality at all, and is as colorless as Shakespeare himself seems to have chosen to be. Yet nothing could be more colorful than the Second Part of *Faust*, which is peopled by an astonishing array of monsters, grotesque devils, and classical ghosts.

A contrast between Shakespeare and Goethe demonstrates that in each—but in very different ways—we can better find the work in the person, than we can discover that banal entity, the person in the work. Goethe to many of his contemporaries, seemed to be a mortal god. Shakespeare, so far as we know, seemed an affable, rather ordinary fellow, who aged early and became somewhat withdrawn. Yet Faust, though Mephistopheles battles for his soul, is hardly worth the trouble unless you take him as an idea and not as a person. Hamlet is nearly every-idea-in-one, but he is precisely a personality and a person.

Would Hamlet be so astonishingly persuasive if his father's ghost did not haunt him? Falstaff is more alive than Prince Hal, who says that the devil haunts him in the shape of an old fat man. Three years before composing the final *Hamlet*, Shakespeare invented Falstaff, who then never ceased to haunt his creator. Falstaff and Hamlet may be said to best represent the work in the writer, because their influence upon Shakespeare was prodigious. W. H. Auden accurately observed that Falstaff possesses infinite energy: never tired, never bored, and absolutely both witty and happy until Hal's rejection destroys him. Hamlet too has infinite energy, but in him it is more curse than blessing.

Falstaff and Hamlet can be said to occupy the roles in Shakespeare's invented world that Sancho Panza and Don Quixote possess in Cervantes's. Shakespeare's plays from 1610 on (starting with *Twelfth Night*) are thus analogous to the Second Part of Cervantes's epic novel. Sancho and the Don overtly jostle Cervantes for authorship in the Second Part, even as Cervantes battles against the impostor who has pirated a continuation of his work. As a dramatist, Shakespeare manifests the work in the writer more indirectly. Falstaff's prose genius is revived in the scapegoating of Malvolio by Maria and Sir Toby Belch, while Falstaff's darker insights are developed by Feste's melancholic wit. Hamlet's intellectual resourcefulness, already deadly, becomes poisonous in Iago and in Edmund. Yet we have not crossed into the deeper abysses of the work in the writer in later Shakespeare.

No fictive character, before or since, is Falstaff's equal in self-trust. Sir John, whose delight in himself is contagious, has total confidence both in his self-awareness and in the resources of his language. Hamlet, whose self is as strong, and whose language is as copious, nevertheless distrusts both the self and language. Later Shakespeare is, as it were, much under the influence both of Falstaff and of Hamlet, but they tug him in opposite directions. Shakespeare's own copiousness of language is well-nigh incredible: a vocabulary in excess of twenty-one thousand words, almost eighteen hundred of which he coined himself. And of his word-hoard, nearly half are used only once each, as though the perfect setting for each had been found, and need not be repeated. Love for language and faith in language are Falstaffian attributes. Hamlet will darken both that love and that faith in Shakespeare, and perhaps the Sonnets can best be read as Falstaff and Hamlet counterpointing against one another.

Can we surmise how aware Shakespeare was of Falstaff and Hamlet, once they had played themselves into existence? *Henry IV, Part I* appeared in six quarto editions during Shakespeare's lifetime; *Hamlet* possibly had four. Falstaff and Hamlet were played again and again at the Globe, but Shakespeare knew also that they were being read, and he must have had contact with some of those readers. What would it have been like to discuss Falstaff or Hamlet with one of their early readers (presumably also part of their audience at the Globe), if you were the creator of such demiurges? The question would seem nonsensical to most Shakespeare scholars, but then these days they tend to be either ideologues or moldy figs. How can we recover the uncanniness of Falstaff and of Hamlet, when they now have become so familiar?

A writer's influence upon himself is an unexplored problem in criticism, but such an influence is never free from anxieties. The biocritical problem (which this series attempts to explore) can be divided into two areas, difficult to disengage fully. Accomplished works affect the author's life, and also affect her subsequent writings. It is simpler for me to surmise the effect of *Mrs. Dalloway* and *To the Lighthouse* upon Woolf's late *Between the Acts*, than it is to relate Clarissa Dalloway's suicide and Lily Briscoe's capable endurance in art to the tragic death and complex life of Virginia Woolf.

There are writers whose lives were so vivid that they seem sometimes to obscure the literary achievement: Byron, Wilde, Malraux, Hemingway. But most major Western writers do not live that exuberantly, and the greatest of all, Shakespeare, sometimes appears to have adopted the personal mask of colorlessness. And yet there are heroes of literature who struggled titanically with their own eras—Tolstoy, Milton, Victor Hugo—who nevertheless matter more for their works than their lives.

There are great figures—Emily Dickinson, Wallace Stevens, Willa Cather—who seem to have had so little of the full intensity of life when compared to the vitality of their work, that we might almost speak of the work in the work, rather than even of the work in a person. Emily Brontë might well be the extreme instance of such a visionary, surpassing William Blake in that one regard.

I conclude this general introduction to a series of literary bio-critiques by stating a tentative formula or principle for gauging the many ways in which the work influences the person and her subsequent, later work. Our influence upon ourselves is always related to the Shakespearean invention of self-overhearing, which I have written about in several other contexts. Life, as well as poetry and prose, is overheard rather than simply heard. The writer listens to herself as though she were somebody else, and the will to change begins to operate. The forces that live in us include the prior work we have done, and the dreams and waking visions that evade our dismissals.

HAROLD BLOOM

Introduction

Camus, only forty-six when he died in a car crash, nevertheless seems to have completed a life's work, his fictions and dramas. If he has a work that transcends the status of a period-piece, it would be *The Myth of Sisyphus* (1943), though that ambitious essay is destroyed when juxtaposed to Kierkegaard or Nietzsche.

My friend Paul de Man, who had a kind of disinterested interest in Camus, told me once (it must be forty years ago) that Camus gave him an authentic sense of the fragility of the human condition but little impression of any cognitive strength. In 2003, that seems not unfair: I cannot recall *any* idea, even in *The Myth of Sisyphus*, that has retained its freshness. As for our condition being vulnerable, Camus doubtless catches the tension of the German Occupation and the Liberation years, but that is merely to be the moralist-as-reporter. Try interpolating any essay by Montaigne into your rereading of *The Myth of Sisyphus*. The fully achieved voice of Montaigne will render you deaf to Camus's fragile intensities.

It is the sorrow of most writing that it must dwindle into just such period-pieces, like films we loved when young that cannot bear reseeing. I don't think I could reread *The Stranger* and *The Plague* again, and I have just barely made my way back through *The Myth of Sisyphus*. *The Rebel* is so dated that I scarcely can try to get into it.

Camus stands or falls by his defense of "the absurd" in *The Myth of Sisyphus*. Whether there is any coherence in this concept of the Absurd

1

is now quite disputable. Camus thought his "absurd" was an anti-
nihilism, balanced between suicide and religion. That is a pretty broad
"absurd," dwelled in, after all, by every secularist I know who is not
addicted to self-slaughter.

The best defense I know of Camus is by Paul de Man, who felt an
affinity for what was salutary in the spirit of Camus. Here is Paul de Man
reviewing Camus's *Notebooks 1942–1951*:

> His particular moral sense, one of protectiveness, is
> rooted in this awareness of man's "nakedness." But this
> nakedness has nothing in common with "physical freedom."
> A reconciliation of the two notions is not easily achieved; it
> comes about only in the highest manifestations of art or
> thought. And the first step in such a reconciliation always
> involves the renunciation of the naive belief in a harmony at
> the beginning of things. When Camus characterizes Greek
> art as a "benign barrenness" (*un dénuement souriant*), he does
> not seem to realize that this equilibrium is the final outcome,
> and not the starting point, of a development that is anything
> but "natural." Rooted in a literal and physical notion of unity,
> his own thought falls apart, on the one hand, in a seductive
> but irresponsible dream of physical well-being and, on the
> other, in a protective moralism that fails to understand the
> nature of evil. Camus never ceased to believe that he could
> shelter mankind from its own contingency merely by
> asserting the beauty of his own memories.

I have called that a "defense" but intellectually it is a damnation.
When I think of Camus, my principal affect is a certain wistfulness. He
was a better man than he was a writer or thinker: as a leader in the
Resistance he edited its newspaper, *Combat*. In 1957, he received the
Nobel Prize for Literature. Like so many Nobel laureates, he will vanish
as a writer. The aesthetic is unforgiving: it demands achieved beauty and
cognitive strength. Camus will be absorbed by history, and it will not be
the history of literature.

NEIL HEIMS

Biography of Albert Camus

"Once again I look, as I have for years, at the designs that the foam and the wake make on the surface of the water, this lace which is incessantly made and unmade."

—*Albert Camus*[1]

THE THIRTIES IN ALGIERS

If ever there was a time when history was gathering itself to show its might, the vanity of human action, and the insignificance of the individual, it was the 1930s. The decade began, however, with just the opposite indications. Whether on the political right or on the left, people accepted that through concerted effort and collective activity the great processes of history could be influenced, vexing conditions altered and the lives of individuals improved. To many, the Soviet Union seemed to be a beacon of progressive and humane activity, a place of possibility. The crimes of Stalinism were largely unknown, and the rhetoric of Soviet communism, unlike the violent master race propaganda of Nazi Germany, was framed in terms of humanity, equality, generosity, justice, and the amelioration of brutality. By the end of the decade, the idea that the good of the individual was the proper end of collective endeavor had been defeated. Weimar gave way to Berlin, republican Spain to Franco, the Popular Front to Vichy, workers' collectives to gulags. The surviving doctrine taught that the individual's proper function was to serve as an abstraction, whether a Folk State, a Socialist Future or Defeating Fascism, that the "end justified the means," no matter how brutal the means. For Albert Camus the decade and its culmination, the Second World War, served as a refiner's fire.

Camus's self-perception and self-regard depended on his encounters with and responses to the great movements and forces of history, to challenges which seemed inevitable and apparently outside individual control, like fascism, war and the tuberculosis that plagued him all his life. His experience of poverty and of the race discrimination he saw practiced against Arabs in Algeria gave him a consciousness of injustice and a conviction that the values and customs which supported injustice and exploitation had to be replaced. He joined the Communist Party. Certainly, the issues of poverty, workers' rights, and race were significant factors in his decision.

"I've joined the Communist Party," he wrote to his friend Claude de Fréminville in the fall of 1935, "where I will work loyally as a soldier, not in the leadership committee. My skills will be used in journalism for *La Lutte Sociale* [the Communist Party magazine, *Social Struggle*] and in Marxist classes, etc. We must experience the hardship and triumphs of Communism ..." But for Camus, more was involved. He concludes the sentence saying, "and in one year I'll take stock." (Todd, 37) He had in fact written Fréminville a year earlier resisting urgings to join the party, which he characterized as "tying yourself to a credo," (Todd, 28) saying that "I have a deep-seated attitude against religion, and for me, communism is nothing if not a religion. To belong would mean to force myself to hide my other beliefs.... If I went toward Communism ... I'd put my vitality, intelligence and power into it, I might put my talent and soul, but not all my heart." (Todd, 29) The date is uncertain, but by August 1935, he had put his reservations aside and joined the party.

One of the reasons for his decision to use the Communist Party as the vehicle for ameliorative activism was the influence of his hero-teacher Jean Grenier, with whom he stayed in touch throughout his life. Grenier led discussion groups on communism, in his home, for the young who gathered around him at the university, arguing that "if you're going to do philosophy, politics is necessary." (Todd, 37) Grenier was not a doctrinaire thinker or a man of narrow interests. Besides *Les Iles*, *The Islands*, an appreciation of the spiritual influences of places like islands and deserts, Grenier had written "An Essay against the Orthodox

Mind." Camus saw joining the Communist Party as an exercise in his own individual development, "as a springboard and asceticism that prepares the ground for more spiritual activities.... it's a way to shirk false idealism and mechanical optimism, and establish a situation where man can rediscover his sense of eternity." (Todd, 37–38) He soon rejected the tyranny of eternity, preferring the liberty of the present. But his lifelong quest to establish, through his work, a spiritual orientation and a moral foundation in a world without God or eternity is apparent. At the root of this quest was a defining refusal to compromise with evil for the alleged sake of good. In Camus's thought, meaning comes only from human acts. Camus's work reveals his great and on-going argument with Dostoevsky, his struggle against the assertion that without God, anything is permitted, and there is no basis for morality, goodness or even decency.

Once in the Communist Party, Camus was made Secretary General of the Algerian Cultural Center. (Todd, 60) His task was to give the cultural life of the city a consciousness of the issues and values that would advance the causes the party supported. At the Algiers Circle of Progress meetings, when the party line favored forging an alliance with the native Algerian Moslems, he spoke with members of the Islamic Studies group. (Todd, 39) In April of 1936, he addressed a crowd at the Stella Cinema. According to the police report of the event,

> M. Camus gave the history of the Popular Front movement, saying that in order to understand the Popular Front, one must understand Europe's current situation, with Fascist Germany's violence, Fascist Italy's [Ethiopian] colonial war, and Nationalist Japan's effort to make China into a colony. (Todd, 40)

Camus devised and supervised a number of programs at the Culture Center, often speaking himself about politics and culture. In 1937, when André Gide published *Retour de l'URSS*, an account of his disillusionment with the Soviet Union, the central office of the party vetoed Camus's plan to present a debate about it at the Center. He went ahead, nevertheless, and in June of that year several members of the party accused him of various managerial and ideological malefactions, including embezzling funds from the Center. He was also censured for staging Ben Jonson's comedy *Epicocene, or The Silent Woman*, not among the party-sanctioned plays like Gorky's *Lower Depths*, which he also staged, but actually a serious, although comically devised, meditation on the role of women and the vagaries of gender. (Todd, 60–61)

Until he became troublesome to the party, Camus had been very busy doing its business. Besides running the Culture Center, speaking at meetings, and editing *La Lutte Sociale*, Camus had played a significant part in organizing and running *Le Théâtre du travail*, The Workers' Theater, dedicated to working class issues presented in a revolutionary format. In the leaflet announcing the theatre, Camus wrote,

> A Workers' Theater is being organized in Algiers thanks to a collective and disinterested initiative. This Theater is conscious of the artistic value inherent in mass literature, wishes to prove that art can sometimes profit by moving out of its ivory tower, and believes that a sense of beauty is inseparable from a certain sense of humanity.... The Workers' Theater ... is not concerned with originality. Its aim is to reinstate certain human values.... (Bree, 33)

The theater was to operate in such a way that it would "avoid all the "commonplaces" of propaganda," and that it might go beyond conventional and comfortable methods of play production. First efforts included an adaptation of André Malraux's *Le Temps du Mépris (Days of Wrath)*, performed on the dock of a waterfront café by amateur actors, and the collectively created choral drama, *Revolte dans les Asturies*, which was published in 1936, but whose performance was forbidden by the mayor of Algiers, Augustin Rozis. The play concerned the revolt of the miners of Oviedo, which had been brutally suppressed two years earlier. The characters of the play are based on the miners themselves. The play is designed not for a proscenium stage but to be performed around the spectators who thus find themselves in the middle of the action, not in front of it, and according to seating, each seeing the action from a different perspective. The force opposing the miners was represented by a voice over a loud-speaker, which argued with the live actors. (Bree, 30–33)

Revolte was the only work of collective authorship the theater attempted, but the group did present an adaptation of Fyodor

Dostoevsky's *The Brothers Karamazov* and a production of Maxim Gorky's *The Lower Depths*. Soon, however, the members of the theater began to differ about its function. Some argued theater ought to deliver social messages. Camus argued for "good theater" not propaganda or orthodoxy, and his position prevailed. After his separation from the party, he stayed with the theater and *Le Théâtre du travail* became *Le Théâtre de l'equipe*, The Team Theater, and continued to present plays until 1939. Production of Camus's adaptation of Aeschylus' *Prometheus Bound*, J. M. Synge's *The Playboy of the Western World* and works by Alexander Pushkin, and Gide constituted Camus's first association with theater as playwright, actor and director, (Bree, 33–34) but not his last. On the very day of his death, Pierre Moinot an assistant to André Malraux, then the Minister of Culture in de Gaulle's government, wrote to Camus that the appropriation of 100 million (old) francs had been approved for an experimental theater company Camus had been named to run. Shortly before, in a television interview Camus had said,

> Why am I in the theater? I've often wondered. The only answer I can find up to now will no doubt seem to you discouraging in its banality: simply because the theater is one of the spots in the world where I am happiest. (Bree, 64)

Just as the date Camus joined the Communist Party is not certain, so both the date and the process of his exit are also inexactly known. But by 1937, and perhaps as early as 1936, Camus was no longer a member of the party. Besides his disinclination to put party discipline above intellectual inquiry, the most specific reason for the separation was his outspoken opposition to a shift in the party's line on native Algerians and colonialism, an issue that would always haunt him. From supporting Arab nationalism, as part of popular front strategy, the party moved to condemning Algerian Moslem nationalists as "fascist" when it (the Communist Party) allied itself with the Radical Socialist Party whose policies were colonialist. (Lottman, 156) Camus's break with the communists did not, thus, signal a change in his values or concerns. He remained dedicated to the socialist ideas of social and economic justice and an end to colonial exploitation throughout his life. Nevertheless, he would be vilified by many dogmatic leftists as the Cold War intensified in the 1950s for his evenhanded and pacifist condemnation of both East and West and for refusing to simplify the complexities of the French-Algerian conflict or his troubled response to it.

The 1930s are also the years during which Camus became a writer. He worked on a novel, *Le Quartier pauvre*, *The Poor District*, which he did not finish. His second novel, 1935, unpublished until after his death, began as *La Vie heureuse*, *The Happy Life*, but became *La Mort heureuse*, *The Happy Death*. Much of his own experience went into it. He had been a lively, active, athletic, sexually vital young man. Tuberculosis was a blow to his mortality and an enemy against which he rallied his creative force. It made him live in relation to death as well as to life. Each time it struck it debilitated and suffocated him. His experience of poverty and injustice also contributed to his art, as did the wretched early marriage to Simone Hié, who he abandoned and which left a bitter pain to goad his creativity. His marital distress also gave weight to his experience of Prague, which figures in the novel. During the final days of his first marriage, Simone and Camus traveled through Austria with Yves Burgeois, Camus's friend and English teacher, and then stopped in Prague. It was there Camus learned of Simone's sex for morphine arrangement with a physician in Algiers by seeing a letter of hers from him. The North African sun, landscape and water, which had nurtured him up through manhood also figured in his art. Like Spain for Jake Barnes in Ernest Hemingway's *The Sun Also Rises* they buoy up his sense of living gladness, and offer an antidote to the bleak claustrophobia of Europe that oppresses his hero in the novel and of which Camus himself often complained.

Camus combined these elements in a story of a crime of robbery and murder and its aftermath, but unlike Dostoevsky who uses a story of crime and punishment to convince us of the necessity for belief in an eternal God, the aftermath Camus develops includes neither punishment resulting from a relentless detective or from self-laceration. Rather Camus's novel explores how his crime leads his hero through a consequent reaction of anguish, fear and nausea, to a consciousness of the void within himself, which cannot be filled in the darkness of Europe. His hero leaves Prague, the city to which he had fled after the crime, and returns to the sun and the sea of North Africa and to a sense of the importance of present experience. In the end the hero, Patrice Mersault, who bears almost the same name as the renowned hero of Camus's next novel, *The Stranger*, dies a happy death. He experiences, not salvation, redemption, the presence of God, or the possibility of eternity, but an obliteration of self within the cosmic. Camus was unsatisfied with the novel. Nevertheless, in it he expressed the germ of his philosophy and the landscape of his imagination. In February of 1938, he wrote to Francine Faure, who would become his second wife in 1940,

> I've been writing nonstop—I can tell you, can't I?—a whole novel, which I finished recently [*La Mort heureuse*].... Only it was all written in exasperation, carried inside me for hours to be written down only in the evenings. Now, despite compliments from Grenier and Heurgon, what they say clearly shows it's a failure, too herky-jerky to be artistic.
>
> For some days, that was a serious blow, as I had thought of it as my last chance, but I was wrong, and now things are better....
>
> Last year I was afraid to take myself seriously but now I'm no longer playing games and I want to be a writer. (Todd, 70–71)

Camus did, however, use some of the material from *La Mort heureuse*: his youth in Belcourt, recollections of his mother, his grandmother's death, the neediness of an old man in a café, his own youthful travels. These themes comprise a volume of five autobiographical essays, *L'Envers et l'endroit*, *The Wrong Side and the Right Side*, which, appearing in 1937, was his first published book.

As if to balance these essays of witness to pain and solitude, which evoke the vacancy of the experience of life, Camus followed *L'Envers et l'endroit* with *Noces*, *Nuptials*, a collection of four lyrical essays celebrating the beauty of the world and the natural and spontaneously meaningful affinity between human beings and the landscapes which support and nourish us.

This antithetical pairing is not coincidental. Camus organized his work, and mapped it out in a series of sequences, each series consisting of several works of varying genres related thematically and by the investigation of particular issues. Here is Camus's scheme, an entry from his *Notebooks*, dated June 17, 1947:

First series. Absurd: *The Stranger—The Myth of Sisyphus—Caligula* and *The Misunderstanding* [*Le Malentendu*].

Second series. Revolt: *The Plague* (and appendices*)—The Rebel*—Kaliayev [*The Just Assassins* [*Les Justes*]].

Third series. Judgement—The First Man.

Fourth series. Love sundered (or Anguished love): the Stake—On Love—The Charmer (or The Seductive One)

Fifth series. Creation Corrected or The System: Big novel + great meditation + unplayable play. (*Notebooks*, 158)

In addition to forging a career as a writer of literature, Camus was active throughout his life as a journalist, most notably as the underground editor of the clandestine French Resistance newspaper *Combat* during the Second World War. His earliest newspaper work was as a music columnist for *La Presse libre* and as a reporter for *Oran Matin* in Algeria in the early thirties. He began writing for *Alger-Republicain*, a paper begun in 1938 to combat the growing climate of fascism and anti-semitism in Algiers when the paper was established. There he met and worked with Pascal Pia, a man who would be of great importance to him, to whom he dedicated *The Myth of Sisyphus*. Pia in his youth had been a poet, a friend of André Malraux, had worked on several left wing or communist front daily newspapers and, like Camus, his father had been killed in the First World War. Later, during the Second World War and the German occupation of France he was a member of the Resistance and recruited Camus to be his co-editor on *Combat*.

Starting as a reporter for *Alger-Republicain*, Camus soon was writing a regular column, *The Reading Room*, reviewing books, writing about the arts and reflecting on the news. In March 1939, he began a series of eleven articles on Kabylia, a green, mountainous region of Algiers inhabited by Berbers. "Poverty in Kabylia" was written over a period of four months and described the life of the people, their exploitation and suffering. To defuse the indignation Camus's series aroused, the Governor General of Algiers visited Kabylia soon afterwards, but it was August of 1939 and world events overshadowed Algerian issues.

BEGINNINGS

Albert Camus, the son of Lucien Auguste Camus and Catherine Sintes, was born in a small whitewashed bungalow in the village of St. Paul, just north of the small town of Mondovi in Algeria on November 7, 1913. His mother was of Spanish descent, his father French. Lucien Auguste worked in the wine cellars of the firm of *Jules Ricôme et fils*, supervising the pressing of grapes and the shipping of the wine. In 1913, when Albert, his second son, was seven months old, *Pere* Camus was drafted into the French Army to fight in the First World War, and died on October 11, 1914 from wounds received during the Battle of the Marne. He was twenty-eight. His wife, Catherine, four years his senior, one of nine children, illiterate throughout her life, partly deaf, and hampered by a speech impediment, was thirty-one when Albert Camus was born. Impoverished by the death of her husband, she moved with her two children into her mother's apartment, which occupied the top floor of the building with two other apartments in Belcourt, a lower working class waterfront district of Algiers. For the duration of the war, she worked sorting cartridges in a munitions factory; after the war she was a cleaning woman and laundress. There was neither electricity nor running water in their apartment. Camus, his mother and his older brother Lucien lived in one of three rooms, Camus and Lucien sharing one bed until Albert was seventeen. Two of his uncles, one, Etienne, a barrel maker, occupied another room, which served also as the dining room, and his grandmother occupied the third room. The common toilet for the three apartments was in the hall and evacuated into a ditch outside. Camus's grandmother, also named Catherine was a domineering, even cruel woman. She supplanted her daughter, who was unable to stand up to her, and raised the boys harshly, frequently hitting them with a *nerf de boeuf*, a whip made with the dried ligament of a bull's neck. Camus lived under these circumstances until he moved in with his aunt and uncle, Antoinette and Gustave Acault in 1930, when he was seventeen and recuperating from his first bout with tuberculosis.

His early and formative life of poverty was not a poor life, Camus reports. Belcourt provided a waterfront and a beach. As a boy and as a young man, Camus had a band of friends and the diverse and colorful neighborhoods of Algiers, including the Casbah, the factory district and the docks to explore. He was an excellent swimmer, and the Algerian sun provided an immediate experience of an ongoing and sensuous present. "Poverty," he wrote

> was never a misfortune for me: it was always counterbalanced by the richness of light. And, because it was free from bitterness, I found mainly reasons for love and compassion in it. Even my rebellions at the time were illuminated by this light. They were essentially—and I think I can say it without misrepresentation—rebellions in favor of others. It is not certain that my heart was inclined to this kind of love. But circumstances helped me and, to correct my natural indifference, I was placed half way between poverty and the sun. Poverty prevented me from judging that all was well in the world and in history, the sun taught me that history is not everything. [Preface *L'Envers et l'endroit.*] (Bree, 61)

Belcourt had a library, movie theaters and cafes; the young played together when they were children and preened, pranced and flirted when they became teenagers.

More deeply formative was the relationship he had with his mother which would reverberate throughout his life and his art. She seems to have been a sweet and gentle woman, intimidated by her family and emotionally confined. When she took a lover, her brother broke up the relationship. Camus longed for her affection, but was frustrated in his longing. Throughout his life he was devoted to her.

As a boy, Camus attended the *Ecole Communale.* Because his father had been killed in the war Albert was a *pupille de la nation* and thus entitled to a small annual stipend for school supplies. He was a very good student from the start, particularly shining in literature. When he was ten years old and in the *cours moyen, 2e anee* (comparable to the fifth grade in the United States), his teacher was Louis Germain, the sort of teacher who is the stuff of legend: dedicated, demanding and inspiring. He recognized the extraordinary in Camus, and on a special visit to their apartment, convinced the family to allow Albert to continue his education at the *Lycee*, rather than leave school and, like his brother Lucien and boys of his station in general, find a job. He helped the boy prepare for a scholarship examination, and, the next year Camus entered the *Lycee Bugeaud*, the larger and less exclusive of the two high schools in Algiers. It was disparagingly known as the Jewish school, and located near the Moslem quarters.

Camus was a lively boy during his high school years, outstanding in literature and philosophy, average in math, confident in his anti-religious stance, but rowdy in school and often punished for it. As in his earlier schooling, he found a teacher who recognized and cultivated his talent and whom he admired, the philosopher Jean Grenier, to whom he later dedicated *L'Homme Revolté*, *The Rebel*. Writing about Grenier's book, *Les Iles*, *The Islands*, at the time, Camus said: "He is completely in [*Les Iles*] and the admiration and love that I feel for him are growing.... Will I ever know how much I owe him?" (Todd, 19) Camus was not a withdrawn, alienated intellectual young man, however. He was devoted to soccer and played it with great enthusiasm, taking quite a few blows. As a youth, before his illness, he was athletic and team oriented. Throughout his life, he was known for being a good dancer and effortlessly successful with women. Unlike his more financially secure schoolmates, he did not take off during the summer vacations; among other jobs, he worked at an ironmonger's shop and as a clerk for a maritime broker.

In 1930, when he was seventeen Camus had a fever and chills and began vomiting blood. It was his first encounter with tuberculosis, a life-long affliction. He lived with it and struggled against it, forcing himself to be the stronger, insisting on life as tuberculosis kept drawing him towards death. Camus's struggle to choose between life and death as it is formulated in *The Myth of Sisyphus* through the question of suicide was a philosophical problem rooted in his own painful experience.

The treatment for tuberculosis before antibiotics, artificial pneumothorax, was primitive and painful. It involved injecting air between the chest wall and the lung, forcing the lung to collapse. During the period of rest imposed upon the lung by this blow the tubercular lesions were supposed to heal. This procedure was repeated every few weeks, and x-rays were taken to monitor the treatment. After hospitalization, paid for by the State since Camus was a war orphan, he moved from his grandmother's apartment to stay in his own room with his aunt and uncle, the Acaults. His uncle Gustave was a butcher, a raconteur, something of an anarchist politically, and a cultivated man with a library in his home which included works by Voltaire, Honore de Balzac, Victor Hugo, Emile Zola, Paul Valery, Anatole France and James

Joyce. Living with the Acaults, Camus was well cared for, a sufficiency of steak and literature available to him. His uncle's liberality, nevertheless, extended only so far, and when Albert at nineteen wanted to bring young women home to spend the night, his uncle refused; Camus moved out to live "almost alone, penniless, and uncertain." (Todd, 25) Relations between the Acaults and Camus suffered a temporary lapse until 1934 when Camus married Simone Hié and his uncle "gave him a little money and lent him his Citroen." (28)

Camus was absent from the Lycée from December 1930 until October 1931 when he returned, repeated his last year, and passed the *bac*, the exam required of all French students for admission to university. His years at the University of Algiers, 1932 through 1936, were important years for him. He continued his relationship with Jean Grenier, who now was teaching philosophy there. Grenier introduced him to the pre-Socratic philosophers and to Saint Augustine. He made friends with a group of student artists and intellectuals, whose orientation was leftist bohemian. They were *for* the oppressed, *for* the working people, *for* the Arabs, and committed to the end of oppression and exploitation in all its forms. So was he then and throughout his life; this engagement constituted the substance of all his work. He and his crowd were inclined to scorn the fetters of bourgeois values in matters of sex and friendship, regarding honesty as more authentic than conventionality or *politesse*. Writing to his friend Claude de Fréminville of his negative reaction to some poems Fréminville had shown him, Camus said, "You understand ... why I am not afraid to tell you the truth, because the real Fréminville will love me more if I'm sincere." (Todd, 24) He praised his friend Max-Pol Fouchet, after Camus told him that he had wooed and won Fouchet's fiancee, Simone Hié because the news did not seem to disturb him. But their friendship did, nevertheless, cool. (Todd, 25, 33)

Camus's marriage to Simone Hié in 1934 lasted a year. She was a glamorous, mysterious young woman, beautiful, sexually free and moody. Her mother was an ophthalmologist who had given her daughter a morphine injection for menstrual cramps when the girl was fourteen, and Simone Hié continued to inject herself with morphine obtained by using prescriptions she stole from her mother or by such sexual relations with physicians who gave her morphine, as the one Camus discovered in Prague. He claimed he did not know of her drug habit before their marriage, and he tried to wean her from her addiction, unsuccessfully, afterwards. Often high, she was neither conventional nor stable. She spent time in hospitals because of her habit. He was jealous of the male attention she attracted. When the combined burdens of her behaviors became overwhelming, he left her.

THE CONFLICT EMBODIED IN MONOGAMY

Camus was a man who had many women in his life, as lovers, friends and co-workers. He was a seducer, and was fascinated by and identified with the figure of Don Juan. He was quite jealous of the women he saw, although he maintained his own right to promiscuity. After he and Simone returned from Prague, he went to live with his brother Etienne and she went back to her mother's house. It was not until four years later when he was planning to marry again that he got a formal divorce, but immediately on parting, they had little to do with each other. She married a doctor, remained a user of narcotics and died in 1970. Occasionally she got in touch with him, asking for help. Shortly before his death he was trying to get her a job in his publisher's office.

As was usual for him, Camus had several girlfriends simultaneously; most knew he was not interested in marriage and domesticity. They knew about each other and often were each other's friends. Sometimes one introduced another to him or discussed whether or not to sleep with him. Yvonne Duclair, for example, was a graduate student at the University in Algiers in 1939 and a substitute teacher of philosophy at a girls' *lycée*. Lucette Meurer, another of Camus's girlfriends introduced them on the terrace of an outdoor café. (Todd, 96) Camus often worked with the women with whom he had liaisons, in the Resistance, on newspapers or in the theater. When he was leaving his job at *the Institut de Meteorologie* [the weather bureau] to work on *Alger-Republicain*, he let Christiane Galindo, whom he began to see after the break up with Simone, know, in case she wanted to replace him there. (Lottman, 175) (Her brother Pierre, a good friend of Camus was in part a model for Meursault in *The Stranger*.) With Yvonne he discussed Russian philosophers, and she participated in the activities of the *Théâtre de l'equipe*.

He also confided in women, speaking of his work and his inner workings. To Christiane Galindo, for example, he wrote in July 1939:

> I just this minute finished *Caligula*, and it's unbearable,
> because I feel that I can do better than that, and I must
> rewrite it. I'm moving on Saturday and I'll start my novel at
> my mother's home, and all that will take a lot of time…. I'm
> afraid to see F. again; I want to see her, but I don't want to get
> back together in any way, because I've got better things to do.
> Maybe it's better just to let everything die. For my works, I
> need freedom of mind, and freedom, period. (Todd, 95)

His novel is *The Stranger*, which he had begun sketching in his notebook
a year earlier. "F." is the Francine Faure whom he will marry in
December 1940. Their marriage will continue, formally, with long
intervals of alienation or separation, until his death. It will be defined by
his promiscuity and long-term liaisons and by her periods of depression,
a suicide attempt and hospitalization. She was a very beautiful woman, a
dancer and a classical pianist—she loved Bach—a mathematician and a
teacher. She is said to have moved with suppleness and natural elegance.
Weeks before his death, during the Christmas holidays at their home in
Lourmarin in France, before leaving for Paris—where he anticipated
seeing several of the women with whom he had long-term involvements—
he told Francine, "You are my sister, you resemble me, but one shouldn't
marry his sister." (Todd, 412) The recurring question is why he married
her. Perhaps he really did need to have a domestic or even maternal
figure with whom he could—like Sisyphus repeatedly pushing a stone up
a hill, but never getting to set it there for good—endlessly recapitulate
the pain and frustration of failing to accomplish a wished for connection,
as when a boy, with his mother. The nub of what drew him to her despite
his frequent disinclination to be with her, perhaps lies in the following
entry from his *Notebooks*:

> The moment I saw on her face an expression of pain, her will
> became mine: I was at my ease only when she was satisfied
> with me. (*Notebooks*, 242)

Coming from a strict and protective family, Francine was reserved
and proper, taking offense at dirty jokes or coarse language. Her family
wouldn't allow him to see her unless he promised to marry her. She
wouldn't sleep with him unless he promised to marry her. He promised.

After that he often promised to sacrifice his sexual liberty, but he never did. Throughout their marriage, nevertheless, his becoming faithful seems to have been an end she hoped might be accomplished. (Todd, 271)

His antipathy to marriage, and the difficulty of their relationship were already apparent in the days of their courtship. Frequently when speaking of her to others, he wrote he loved her, but institutional monogamy was entirely antithetical to him, and did not seem to him the proper condition for the expression or exchange of love. "Why must one love few people in order to love a lot?" (Todd, 97) he wrote Francine, who always knew the way he felt, and when they married, he did not promise fidelity. (98) In 1939, he noted,

> .... two or three years ago, I thought I might be allowed to take a chance on normal happiness, like anyone else.... But then I ruined everything. A little while ago, Francine, whose honest heart I love, called me and I agreed once again to try to be a man like any other.... I'd be lying, and Francine would know it, if I said I accepted that without any regrets. I am missing a lot of pleasure and people, but I'm making an effort to accept it. (Todd, 95–96)

Indeed, he had bouts of sexual self-contempt and a longing for asceticism and monasticism. (272) In 1943, not long after marriage, Camus wrote:

> Sexuality leads to nothing; it isn't immoral, but it's unproductive. One can abandon oneself to it when one does not want to produce anything. But only chastity is linked to personal progress. There is a time when sexuality is a victory—when one separates it from moral imperatives—but then it quickly becomes a defeat, and in turn, the only victory which is won over it is chastity.... Uncontrolled sexuality leads to a philosophy of the world's nonsignificance. In contrast, chastity gives back meaning. (Todd, 157)

In the same letter to Yvonne in which he wrote "I want so much to kiss you, and also to turn away," he also said, writing about himself and

Francine: "I'm probably going to waste my life, if common sense is any judge. I mean I'm going to marry F., unless she refuses me." (Todd, 106) She didn't, but their marriage was not the one she wished, nor was it in accord with his disposition, and that made him, when he was true to himself, hurtful to her, and when he was true to her, punitive to himself.

The following entry from his Notebook of November 1942 complicates our vision of Camus, and yet may help to understand him:

> Outside of love, woman is boring, although she doesn't know it. You must live with her and keep silent. Or else sleep with them all and make love. What matters is something else. (*Notebooks*, 42)

How strange an entry from Albert Camus, who is often praised or condemned as the pure conscience of his era! Does he mean it? He was also a man of his era. Contrast it, nevertheless, with this from a letter in July 1938 to Lucette Maurer:

> People attract me insofar as they are impassioned about life and avid for happiness, which is perhaps why I have more women friends than men. (Todd, 98)

Or with this entry from his *Notebook* regarding the world he was creating in *The Plague*: "it's a world without women and thus without air." (*American Journals*, 45) These contradictory utterances, like his marriage and his ambivalent attitudes about sexuality, reveal Camus as a conflicted person whose integrity was the result of a deep struggle and a refusal to disavow one or another of its conflicting elements. Entries in his *Notebooks* suggest both the division and the struggle to discipline a disinclined self. "I have," he writes, "a romantic soul and have always had considerable trouble interesting it in something else." (*Notebooks*, 235) The entries about women may be less jarring, however, if they are seen not only as indicating a conflict in Camus character, but as presenting a fundamental conflict that absorbed his attention in his work as well as in his life.

The passages cited, written four years apart, appear contradictory because they have been generated by differing circumstances. They do not reflect *a priori* attitudes, but responses that refer to something about

Camus rather than about women in general or in particular. When he spoke as a free and unbound man, he related to women with a spontaneous liveliness that perceived women as persons and cultivated their vigor. When, however, he spoke from within the bonds of monogamy, of institutionalization and obligation, boredom was the result because he was cut off from his own authenticity. The demand to conform to a transcendental model undid him. "Let a tiny part of the heart be subject to duty," he wrote in his notebook in October 1949, "and true love is impossible." (*Notebooks*, 219) He makes the same point again in his notebooks with a little parable:

> A man is rewarded officially for a virtue he has practiced instinctively. From that moment on, he practices it consciously: catastrophes. (*Notebooks*, 248)

Camus's apparent ambivalent regard for women, the conflict he felt between sexuality and chastity and his simultaneous capitulation to and defiance of monogamy and marital fidelity, however they may be psychologically rooted, gave him the experience of the philosophical problem his work explores, the conflict between abstraction and particularity, between predetermined structures to which one must adapt or a spontaneous interaction between a person and a present situation, between duty and spontaneity. In his *Notebooks*, he wrote:

> He told her that the love of men was like this, a will and not a grace, and that he had to conquer himself. She insisted that this was not love. (220)

The tension between perceiving the world in terms of abstractions or particulars and of achieving meaningfulness in life by will and action when grace—the unsolicitable and undeserved intervention of divinity into the human sphere—is absent, even impossible, is what he explored in his first series of three works which he called "The Absurds," the novel *The Stranger*, the essay/tract, *The Myth of Sisyphus*, and *Caligula*, a play.

THE ABSURD

In *The Myth of Sisyphus* the problem Camus confronts is suicide. The question of whether or not to kill yourself (or in the case of a tubercular Camus, to surrender to the death that has begun to invade) forces asking the question, Is there reason to live? If there is, what is it? What makes the question fresh is that Camus rejected the traditional imperative for living. Traditionally, the answer is God. God gives meaning and purpose to living because the existence of God bespeaks an existence beyond the realm of our being greater and truer than we can know or perceive, which therefore demands faith. Through faith and a consequent subduing humbleness we can submit our wills and desires to the authority and guidance of this reality. Service and obedience to God and to God's will and laws provide what to live for. By definition, belief in God's existence affirms a realm of purpose and meaning we cannot see but we can approach. The struggle that justifies and gives meaning, direction and limit to our lives, then, is to achieve the transcendental realm, or at least to know that we exist for something beyond ourselves.

The theologies preceding Nietzsche's declaration of God's death scorned the idea that to live for ourselves is either sufficient or meaningful. In fact, it was a prescription for living badly. Only the postulation of a transcendent existence, such theologies argue, can establish and ensure our morality by offering ways to be, to act, and to think. There is a pattern to which we conform. Obviously this paradigm of being and behavior can substitute another term for "God." It can be the Fascist ideal of the *Volk*, the *Reich* or the *Fuehrer*, or it can be the Communist idea of a Workers' State or a Utopian Future as well as an ecclesiastical vision of a Day of Judgment and Eternal Life which can be empowered through our faith. Within any of these models life *has* meaning. Within those systems, too, that meaning often requires the eradication of people who do not profess that faith and who disrupt or contradict that meaning. Mobilization against opposition is often just what principally gives such systems meaning.

In *The Myth of Sisyphus* Camus postulates the world devoid of any templates for meaning. What constitutes the Absurdity of existence is the emptiness at its center, that it is often irrational and unjust, meaningless and temporary. For Camus, the creation which gives meaning inside a world otherwise meaningless is the work of each individual as an individual and teamed with others, not God. Each situation creates its needs; attending to them gives us the opportunity to be human. Camus rejects God and god-like exercises of power for mankind, but clings to the need for virtuous action, and is thus a moralist who forbids himself to construct a moral superstructure. Nevertheless, according to Camus, the world is mankind's to make.

In *The Myth of Sisyphus* Camus accepts the worldview Dostoevsky condemns in *Crime and Punishment*. There is no God, there is void, the world is empty of overriding meaning or purpose, mankind is radically free. Human action creates meaning. Meaningful action, Camus will develop this idea in *The Rebel*, published in 1951 but begun in the early forties, is rebellion against irrationality and meaninglessness. Rebellion, for Camus, is not negation of order but a creative act. Its fundamental principle is that people are meaningful in themselves because we can actualize possibilities. It is with this in mind that Camus wrote in his Notebooks in 1951 that "S[imone] Weil is right; it's not the human being that must be protected, but the possibilities within him." (*Notebooks*, 265)

The second of The Absurd trilogy was the novel, *The Stranger*. For Camus, the Absurd is a category which covers the philosophical, the social and the psychological realms. It indicates a way of understanding and experiencing the world. As *The Myth of Sisyphus* explores the landscape of his thought and the metaphysical implications of the Absurd, so *The Stranger* reveals the landscape of the world of his youth and the social definition of the Absurd. Using the novel as a mirror, in *The Stranger*, Camus explores the triviality of a world in which there is no awareness of the Absurd, of the senselessness of the way people live (except as it is sensed by the narrator, Meursault), yet in which the Absurd prevails, just because conformity to empty convention prevents real feeling and creative thought. Camus establishes Meursault as a central figure, a negative energy, who brings out the absurdity of prevailing viewpoints and actions.

In *The Stranger* Camus drew from persons and situations familiar to him from his life in Algiers and shapes them into the critical vision that gives *The Stranger* the compelling distinctiveness that has made it one of the world's most popular novels and Gallimard's best selling book. Meursault is an amalgam of Camus himself, of his friend Pierre

Galindo, Christiane's brother, and of his friend and editorial and political co-worker, Pascal Pia. The Algerian setting is his home territory. The central incident of the murder is drawn from a story told him at a café, and even the courtroom scenes have the authenticity of being drawn by a man who served as a court reporter on the crime beat of a daily newspaper.

Although *The Stranger* is not an autobiography, there are similarities between Camus and Meursault. Meursault gives an appearance of indifference or detachment, and shows disdain and contempt for convention. His cool exterior covers, at least at the end of the novel, a deep loyalty to his own sense of things. Camus often seemed remote. But he was not, as his work for the Resistance, his political journalism, his third camp pacifism during the Cold War, his subtle responses to the human complexities of Algerian liberation, his activism for Spanish victims of Franco's fascism, and indeed all his literary output demonstrate. So does his marital turmoil. He attempted to discipline himself to adhere to a duty which he believed in although it conflicted with his equally strong belief in the importance of his own liberty. In his Notebooks he defended that liberty with a quotation from Stendhal: "Man is not free not to do what causes him more pleasure than all other possible acts." (*Notebooks*, 236) His long-term out of marriage affairs also demonstrate the depth of his attachments and the strength of his loyalty even without sexual fidelity.

Like Meursault, too, for whom scorn is a liberating emotion, Camus often showed his contempt for those whose vision of life, he thought, was shallow or brutal. In 1939, responding to a comment by a journalist in *La Depeche Algerienne*, impugning the International Brigade that fought on the side of the Spanish Republicans, Camus wrote, "As usual Joseph Prudhomme shows the morality of his pretentious and lying style.... It is terribly tiring to despise people." (Todd, 82) The same year, at the start of the Second World War, Camus expressed his opposition to war in terms of alienation and contempt:

> All have betrayed, those who urged resistance and those who spoke of peace. They are there, as docile and guiltier than the others. And never has the individual been more alone in the face of the lie-making machine. He can still scorn, and use scorn as a weapon. (Lottman, 209)

In 1959, tired and depressed, Camus wrote to his close friend, the poet Rene Char that "it becomes so difficult, so exhausting to struggle when youth fades away, and with it, the strength of insolence and indifference." (Lottman, 642) At the time of their split after the publication of *L'Homme révolté*, *The Rebel*, Jean-Paul Sartre characterized Camus as bearing "a somber self-conceit" (504) and as being pompous. (Todd, 309) And when Czeslaw Milosz, Polish poet and essayist wondered why Camus did not respond to a derisory portrait of him by Simone de Beauvoir in *Les Mandarins*, Camus said, "Because you don't discuss things with a sewer." (325)

Perhaps Meursault's most well-known trait is his cool attitude towards his mother and her death suggested by *The Stranger*'s famous first sentence "Mother died today, or perhaps it was yesterday." Suffering the barrier between them because of her reserve and her illiteracy, Camus, nevertheless, was actively devoted and attentive to his mother. Shortly after learning he had won the Nobel Prize, he sent a telegram to her saying, "Maman, I miss you more than ever." (Todd, 371) It was she who outlived him, saying when told of his death only the stoic words which may cover depths of loss no one else may fathom, "too young." Camus often visited her in Algiers and flew to her sick bed when she was ill. Writing to her in 1959, when she was seventy-seven, he said,

> I hope that you will always stay as young and beautiful and that your heart will remain the best in the world, although it could never change.... I hug you very tightly and kiss you with all my heart. (Todd, 411)

Certainly a declaration which could prejudice no court against him! He dedicated *The First Man*, his last and unfinished novel to her, noting she would never be able to read it.

Caligula, the third work in this series wasn't performed until after the Second World War, and underwent several revisions. *Caligula* represents the power of the absurd: disorder, caprice, insecurity; the nature of the world without God, and the brutality of replacing God with another all encompassing power. In *Caligula*, Camus presents the psychology of a condition, rather than the psychology of the persons, whether victims or victimizers, caught within that condition. As always,

Camus is a moralist. His aim, a moralist's aim, is to warn us that power is capricious, dangerous, and we are always its waiting target. His integrity is marked by a realization that solidarity and rebellion, likely unaccomplishable, nevertheless are our only possibilities. That is why he sets Sisyphus as the emblem of humanity. As well as a limb in the body of his work, *Caligula* represents for Camus the beginning of membership in the intellectual theater world of Paris where he was an actor and a director as well as a playwright. Had he not been killed he would have become the manager/director of a theater subsidized by the French Ministry of Culture.

TAKING HIS PLACE

As a writer Camus fashioned a body of literature using a variety of genres to express the breadth and depth of his concerns especially about moral and political issues. He was true to the active and the contemplative aspects of life, as his work in agitational theater, journalism and his activism within the Algerian Communist Party demonstrate. He allowed each aspect of himself to nourish and influence the other. He approached the world through the mediation of an intellect that refused to be abstracted from experience. In 1939, when he was formulating and integrating philosophies of individual, metaphysical and social existence, he was also responding as he had done throughout the thirties to the actualities of the day. As the world catastrophe became more apparent, his writing became more focused on responding to it. In the highly censored *Le Soir Republicain*, a small paper of opinion, which he and Pascal Pia edited just when the climate of war and suppression was growing, he wrote, "We are deeply pacifistic." (Lottman, 212)

But that curious rift in Camus, emphasized by his marriage, which made one part of him contradict another and cause a division between what he thought and what he did, moved him to enlist for the war—unsuccessfully, because of his health. He seems to have been torn between an allegiance to possibility, on the one hand, and to things as they are, on the other, to the human condition as one finds it and, at the same time, to things as they ought to be. On November 11, 1939, he wrote to his friend Blanche Balin:

You ask me about my position, but you don't need to, because you already know what you want and have already accepted the death of millions of people, consciously or not, in the name of an ideal or inevitability that you're still trying to define. It's painful, no doubt, but you think it is a matter of fate that there is war, and you accept its inevitability.... But war is not inevitable, it could have been avoided, and it still can be at any time. (Todd, 91)

Camus told Grenier that the reason he attempted to join up was "not because he accepted the war, but so as not to use illness as a shield, and also to express solidarity with those who were being called up to fight." (Lottman, 209) To Balin he said, he had tried to enlist because he wanted "to risk my life, although not agreeing with the stakes being offered me." (Todd, 91) He had been weaned on team sports. To world circumstances, as to his tuberculosis, Camus took the same stance, not just a resolve to resist, but a determination to show himself in the same lot as other men and just as capable, despite his infirmity. Later, in the midst of the war and resistance, he entirely abandoned his pacifism. (Todd, 171) At the end of the war, he had also abandoned his opposition to capital punishment, supporting it for collaborators, a position perhaps strengthened by the emotion aroused in him by the execution of his friend, the poet and Resistance fighter René Leynaud by French collaborators in 1944. (*Notebooks*, 273)

In the late thirties in Algeria, Camus and Pia ran *Le Soir Republicain* disregarding government rules, and it was therefore heavily censored until ordered closed. In 1940, Camus moved back and forth between Algiers and nearby Oran, where Francine lived, seeking but failing to find work. Pia had already gone to Paris. There he got a job working on *Paris Soir*, a mass circulation paper short on news and commentary but long on entertainment and gore. He managed to get Camus a job on it as a *secretaire de redaction*, a lay-out man, in charge of make-up and the look of the paper. Pia took care of Camus in Paris, introduced him to friends, including his hero André Malraux. Camus wrote several essays for an anti-fascist weekly, *La Lumiere*, run by some of Pia's friends, and was finishing *The Stranger.*

Camus did not like Paris. It was chilly, damp, dark, and he complained that the faces of the people were too white. It was not at all the place for a young man who'd grown up Algerian, under sun-filled blue, on the Mediterranean and in the heat. But it was a place he could live. Until June of 1940, Paris was complacent; although the war had begun, its first phase was deceptively tranquil. It became known as the "Phony War." The Germans were not seriously moving against France or England. They had aligned with Russia, invaded Poland and were conquering Norway. The French were falsely secure, confident of their defense—a series of fortifications called the Maginot line, whose strength was illusory because the fortification stopped in Belgium. Through this open door the German army marched, seized and occupied Paris and northern France on June 14, 1940. General Charles de Gaulle, whose troops had been defeated, escaped and set up a Free French government in exile in London and then in Algeria. Marshal Philippe Petain, a hero of the First World War established a French government for the Germans in the nominally unoccupied south, with its capital first at Bordeaux and then Vichy. The idea was to save France by collaborating with Germany.

The Nazi invasion caused a great exodus from Paris. *Paris Soir* and its staff, including Camus went to Clermont-Ferand and then to Lyon. Among his coworkers in exile at *Paris Soir* was Janine Thomasset, at the time his lover, she later became the wife of Pierre Gallimard, the nephew of the publisher and then left him for his brother, Michel. All three became life-long, close friends of Camus, and it was Michel who was driving the car in which he and Camus were killed. Francine joined Camus in Lyon to be married on December 3, 1940. Already in September, Camus had written to Fréminiville that "[u]nemployment is widespread and *Paris Soir* in particular has fired half its personnel. They still need me, but it may be only a matter of time." (Todd, 116) A month after his marriage, *Paris Soir* fired Camus too, and he and Francine returned to Oran, and lived with her family.

She found work as a substitute teacher, but Camus could not find any as a writer. Ultimately he got several school jobs, teaching French, history, geography, philosophy, and coaching soccer in a school for Jewish children, who were no longer permitted to attend the public schools. His relations with Francine's family were rocky. He showed a working class disdain for their middle class refinement, deliberately, for example, practicing rough table manners, (Todd, 121) and the strain of marriage irritated him. On his visits to Algiers, he would see Yvonne Duclair, and he wrote to her in January 1941, just a month after his marriage, "I am suffocating here. I am unhappy and I've decided to leave. I don't love anything or anybody and I finally said so to Francine." (123) Camus did have a large group of friends and political comrades, however, in Oran and Algiers, and he spent a good deal of time with them, especially with Christiane Galindo's brother Pierre, whom he said was "the only person here I would be happy to live with." (124) His unhappiness with Francine increased. In June of 1941, he spent many days and nights camping on the beach, and later that summer went camping with Yvonne. He seemed to be in good health; he was in shape and played soccer. He also finished *The Myth of Sisyphus*.

Camus sent the manuscripts of *The Stranger* and *Caligula* to Pascal Pia in April 1941. *The Myth of Sisyphus* was still being typed. Pia, as has already been seen was someone to whom Camus owed a great deal. Pia championed his work, got him jobs that kept him going, provided real working comradeship of the kind they enjoyed in Algiers, and in 1941 he made it his business to get the three books published by Gallimard, the prestigious French publisher. Pia gave the manuscripts of *The Stranger* and *Caligula* to Roland Malraux who gave them to his half brother, André, a friend of Pia's since their youth. André Malraux not only was the author of several important books derived from his life of adventure and political engagement, but as was usual for Gallimard authors, he was employed as a reader and an editor at the firm, as Camus would be, too, for the rest of his life, once he had been published. Pia also spoke to Jean Paulhan about the books and whetted his interest in them. Paulhan was not only a powerful editor at Gallimard; he was well-connected in Parisian literary circles, and welcome in the homes of people who entertained the Nazi brass. Actually, he was a spy for the Resistance. (Todd, 162) Paulhan later became famous when it was revealed that he was the anonymous author of the erotic novel of sado-masochism, *The Story of O*.

In May 1941, Pia wrote to Camus that based on the recommendation of Malraux and Paulhan, Gallimard had accepted *L'Etranger*. Malraux drew up some technical criticisms, (Cf. Todd, 131) but said of the work as a whole:

> *L'Etranger* is obviously an important thing. The power and simplicity of the means which finally force the reader to accept his character's point of view are all the more

remarkable in that the book's destiny depends on whether
this character is convincing or not. And what Camus has to
say while convincing us is not negligible. (131)

Pia was not finished, however. His goal was to get all three works
published, and when it arrived he gave the manuscript of *The Myth of
Sisyphus* to Malraux. After reading it Malraux wrote directly to Camus:

> The link between *Sisyphe* and *L'Etranger* has more
> consequences than I supposed. The essay gives the other
> book its full meaning and, above all, changes what in the
> novel first seemed monotonous and impoverished into a
> positive austerity, with primitive force. (Todd, 133)

Malraux also wrote that he wanted to see the books published "one on
top of the other." (133) He concluded by saying to the young author,

> What matters is that with these two books you will take your
> place among the writers who exist, who have a voice, and
> who will soon have an audience and a presence. There are
> not that many. (134)

In Algeria, Camus did not receive all this with delight. He was
anxious and depressed, alienated in his personal life and struggling with
himself as a writer entering the realm of recognition. Often, he was
troubled by success and seemed as much as he wanted it not to want it.
In his *Notebook* for March 7th 1951, after he enters that he has finished
"the first writing of *The Rebel*" he adds: "Any fulfillment is a bondage. It
obliges one to a higher fulfillment." (*Notebooks*, 270) But the worst
problem was that illness had returned. In February 1942 he was treated
by pneumothorax. In May he was spitting up blood again, and at the end
of the month when he thought he was through with it, he got an even
worse attack of tuberculosis. Toward the end of 1942, Camus reports,
"My youth escapes me; that is being ill." (Lottman, 264) He was, of
course, exhausted, and his in-laws cared for him, and he was grateful to
them. He wanted to go to France, his books were being published there,
and in July, after more illness, Camus' friend Dr. Cviklinski advised he
go to the mountains in France. He and Francine went to Le Panelier, a

hamlet perched at an altitude of 1000 meters in the region of Chambon, where many Jews were secretly sheltered during the war. They stayed in one of its four farms. Camus rested and began to find beauty in the landscape, and treatments in a nearby village of Saint-Etienne, where he observed "the most frightful poverty I have ever seen." (Todd, 153) Meanwhile Gallimard published *The Myth of Sisyphus*, which garnered besides praise and enthusiasm, angry reviews for its "nihilism" and "negativity."

WAR AND RESISTANCE

Camus stayed in France, living in the Massif-Central region to recuperate. Depressed by the bleakness of wartime Lyon, Francine went back to Oran to look for work for them, and Camus was supposed to rejoin her there, but once the allied invasion of North Africa prevented them from traveling they were separated for the duration of the war. Paradoxically the constraints of war allowed Camus the freedom to live like an unmarried man. With the publication of *The Stranger* in 1942 he returned to Paris and began working as a reader and editor at Gallimard, his publisher. He rented a small apartment in a house owned by André Gide who had left Paris for his safety, paying the rent in cash so that Gide might not pay taxes and Camus could keep his whereabouts secret from the Gestapo. (*Notebooks*, 272; Todd, 185) Before returning to Paris Camus had begun working in the *Combat* section of the French Resistance in the Haute-Loire region. (Todd, 193) Among his projects during 1942 and 1943 was a tragedy, *Les Malentendus, Cross Purpose*.

During this period, too, he met and began a liaison with Maria Casarès, the Spanish born French film and stage actress, that would last until his death. Casarès appeared in many of his plays, including *Les Malentendus*, when it was staged in occupied Paris in 1944, *L'Etat de siège, State of Siege* and *Les Justes, The Just Assassins*. She is best remembered for her roles in Marcel Carné's *Children of Paradise*, where she plays the wife of the mime Baptiste, (Jean-Louis Barrault) and in Jean Cocteau's *Orpheus*, where she plays Death. Casarès was the daughter of Santiago Casarès Quiroga, Spanish Prime Minister and Minister of War in Spain in 1936 when General Francisco Franco began a fascist insurrection against Republican Spain. At the age of thirteen, she worked in hospitals helping the Republican cause. The fascist defeat of Spain caused her to flee with her mother to France, where she began to study acting. Camus met her at a private reading of Picasso's play *Le Désir attrapé par la queue*, *Desire Caught by the Tail*. Her beauty, like her temperament was fierce and unconventional, dark, angular and intense. She was unlike Francine. Francine Camus was inward and repressed, diffident and small-voiced. The passionate aspect of her nature was revealed in her suffering. Towards the end of 1949, Camus quotes her in his Notebooks:

> I am a twisted person. The only way I can know my capacity
> for love is from my capacity for anguish. Before suffering, I
> don't know. (*Notebooks*, 233)

In accounts of Camus's life, Francine appears as an intelligent woman, responsible, cultivated, talented, and dependent, with the values of a conventional middle class French housewife, plagued by a depressive illness, the result of jealousy and an unhappy marriage. Casarès was strong-willed and passionate, a woman out in the world on her own. She and Camus attracted each other with a force that their friends noticed and which is apparent in photographs of them, a force apparently absent in his connection with his wife. Like Camus, Casarès had many lovers. (Cf. Todd, 262)

At the end of October 1944, Francine Camus was able to return to France from Algeria. Camus had been living a giddy life, writing *La Peste*, working on *The Rebel*, rewriting *Caligula*, staging *Les Malentendus*, editing *Combat*, the clandestine paper of the Resistance, and spending the nights drinking, talking and dancing in nightclubs with Casarès, Jean-Paul Sartre, Simone de Beauvoir and their circle. It was at dinner at the home of his friends Pierre and Janine Gallimard that he met André Malraux. They took to each other immediately, left together, and spent the night in conversation walking through occupied Paris. With Francine's return and her pregnancy, Camus and Casarès broke off, but the other aspects of Camus's life remained the same. One afternoon in 1948, Camus and Casarès met by chance on the Boulevard Saint Germain, spent the day together and continued to see each other regularly until his death.

Pascal Pia introduced Camus to the Resistance, and in 1942 or 1943, Camus joined and became the co-editor with Pia of the Resistance newspaper *Combat*. He got false identity documents that put his birth year as 1911, identified him as an editor and indicated that his name was Albert Mathé. *Combat* was a rallying point for morale and a vehicle for showing that one could still talk and think freely despite the danger. Its mission was to print and distribute information about the war and the occupation in order to counter German censorship and propaganda. Camus gathered news, wrote editorials, although the anonymity required for safety makes it difficult to identify exactly which pieces are by Camus, and participated in the physical preparation and distribution of the paper.

In Nazi occupied France, resisters and collaborators lived and worked together. Collaborators often were spies and informers. On June 17, 1944, the Gestapo and the pro-German French *milice* raided *Combat's* underground printing plant. In July 1944, Jacqueline Bernard, a courier between the various teams that worked on *Combat* was arrested by the Gestapo. Around that time, one evening, Camus and Casarès were stopped near the Réamur-Sébastapol metro station. He was carrying a layout page with the paper's nameplate. He slipped it to Casarès. He was searched. She only had to show her identity card. They were allowed to go. (Todd, 185–187) Members of the *Combat* group, Camus, Sartre, Beauvoir, Michel, Pierre and Janine Gallimard fled on bicycles to a Paris suburb, Verdolot, for several weeks. The excitement of the Allied advance on Paris drew them back for the final days of the occupation and the explosive nights of the liberation. (Lottman, 324)

In the summer of 1944, United States forces landed in France and were making their way to Paris. Their advance and the consequent weakening of the German army invigorated the Parisians, who began a series of operations, primarily workers' strikes, against the German occupation. As part of that action, in August 1944, Camus along with other members of *Combat* seized the printing plant of a large collaborationist newspaper. (*Notebooks*, 272) *Combat* which had been secretly passed from one person to another in a seven-by-ten-inch format now appeared defiantly out in the open on the embattled street looking like a real newspaper. In the August 24th editorial on the liberation of Paris, Camus caught the intensity of the time, and shaped it, too. He began "The Blood of Freedom" with the archetypal image of Paris, the Seine with its monumental embankment and the historical architecture of power and pride lining it:

> Paris is shooting all her bullets in the August night. In this
> vast setting of stones and waters, all around this river that has
> reflected so much history, the barricades of freedom have
> once more been thrown up. Once more justice must be
> bought with the blood of men.

And he ended looking at the unilluminated sky in a city renowned for its
lights:

> This huge Paris, all black and warm in the summer night,
> with a storm of bombers overhead and a storm of snipers in
> the streets, seems to us more brightly lighted than the City
> of Lights the whole world used to envy us. It is bursting with
> all the fires of hope and suffering, it has the flame of lucid
> courage and all the glow, not only of liberation, but of
> tomorrow's liberty.

"Tomorrow's liberty" is the key phrase. For Camus, getting the Germans
out was the first movement of liberation, but liberation itself demanded
more than that. It meant ending the injustices of economic and cultural
occupation each person is subject to by the machineries of government,
patriotism, finance and labor. Camus was among those who wanted the
liberation of Paris, not to signal the end of resistance, but to be the event
that allowed resistance to become revolution. "The people are under
arms tonight," he wrote, "because they hope for justice for tomorrow....
Paris is fighting tonight ... [n]ot for power, but for justice; not for
politics, but for ethics; not for the domination of France, but for her
grandeur."[1] It was Camus who achieved grandeur.

AFTERMATH

Paris, however, did not make a revolution. After the liberation, General
de Gaulle, head of the French government in exile, representative of the
spirit of the Resistance, became chairman, until 1946, of the provisional
multiparty coalition government composed of Communists, Socialists
and Christian Democrats. It lasted until 1947, when the Fourth French
Republic was established with Jules-Vincent Auriol as president and Paul
Ramadier as the first in a long series of prime ministers. During the

period between liberation and the establishment of the Fourth Republic, competing political and ideological factions jockeyed for power and the implementation of their programs. Under the coalition, which included communist and socialist factions, coal mines, electric and gas utilities, Renault, and the airline industry were nationalized, women were enfranchised, and social security was introduced, all things Camus championed. But French politics were dominated by the trial and punishment of Nazi collaborators, by trouble with the French colonies, which were beginning their wars of national liberation, by a Gaullist desire to restore French power and prestige, by recurring economic issues and by the emerging power struggle between the United States and the Soviet Union. The Fourth French Republic, which lasted until 1958, when General de Gaulle returned to France and was elected president of the Fifth Republic, was an unstable entity and went through a series of crises which toppled government after government.

Nevertheless, what Paris had been for artists in the 1920s, Paris became for intellectuals after the war. It was the center of the ideological debates and disputes that formed the thought and defined the realities of the second half of the 1940s and the ensuing decade. The incipient Cold War was at the core of the arguments, and consequently, so were the problems of choosing sides and of intellectual integrity. Power and the problems—and even the permissibility—of its employment were the determining issues. In a lecture given at the McMillin Theater at Columbia University in New York, during his visit to the United States in 1945, Camus made his position on power clear, "Whenever one judges France or any other country or question in terms of power, one aids and sustains a conception of man which logically leads to his mutilation." (Lottman, 383)

When, at the end of August 1944, *Combat* openly printed the names of its staff, it was revealed that the author of *The Stranger*, widely read and admired, and of *The Myth of Sisyphus*, was a Resistance hero, a person of convictions, not a nihilist. The author of *The Myth of Sisyphus*, far from being an apostle of despair, not only formulated a philosophy of engagement with his classical metaphor, but lived it in action. Camus became emblematic of authenticity, decency and political morality. It was at this time that he most nearly conformed to that image of an intellectual Humphrey Bogart which came to characterize him, and which Neal Oxenhandler depicts this way:

When we visualize Camus, it is the clandestine editor of
Combat who comes to mind. Collar raised, cigarette butt
dangling from the corner of his mouth, he looks ironically
into the middle distance. This aloof man with his dark good
looks has not succumbed to fame nor been daunted by evil.
His face is elongated and somewhat angular, showing his
Spanish heritage. The answer to life's riddle hovers on his
lips. (Oxenhandler, 22)

Camus remained the editor of *Combat*, and the paper was invested
with the reputation for uncompromising integrity similar to his. In 1947,
a lack of funding, a cooling off of the French political climate, and
disagreements over direction caused him to leave. Under Camus's
editorship, *Combat* was reputed to be the best written newspaper ever
published in France. As editor, he supported a socialist revolution and
opposed both the competing world powers, the United States and the
Soviet Union. He saw each as exercising versions of totalitarian control;
he condemned their militarism, especially the American atomic
bombing of Hiroshima and Nagasaki; and he refused to make
philosophical or historical excuses for the brutalities of the Soviet Union
and its satellites. The manifesto Camus wrote for the *Groupes de Liaison
Internationale*, a European association of non-communist leftist
intellectuals allied with an American committee including writers Mary
McCarthy, Alfred Kazin, and Delmore Schwartz, philosopher William
Barrett, and artist-cartoonist Saul Steinberg, which was formed to
support European intellectuals and victims of totalitarianism with
publicity and material aid, reflects his Third Camp stand:

We are a group of men who, in liaison with friends in
America, Italy, Africa, and other countries, have decided to
unite our efforts and our reflections in order to preserve
some of our reasons for living.
These reasons are threatened today by many monstrous
idols, but above all by totalitarian techniques....
These reasons are especially threatened by Stalinist
ideology....
These reasons are threatened also, at a lesser degree it is
true, by American worship of technology. This is not

totalitarian because it accepts the individual's neutrality. But
in its own way it is total because, through films, press and
radio, it has known how to make itself indispensable
psychologically and to make itself loved.... (Lottman, 460)

As an editor at Gallimard, he was similarly participating in the
historical argument by the books he selected to be printed in a series he
edited called *L'Espoir*. Among the works he published were a number of
volumes by Simone Weil, the mystic pacifist anarchist who joined the
loyalists in the Spanish civil war and labored in a factory after graduating
from the Olympian *Ecole Normal Superior*. Her work encompassed social
criticism, philosophy, and theology. Acclaimed by all as brilliant, by
many considered mad, her thought, founded on such principles as
"Official history consists of believing the murderers at their word,"
(Lottman, 374) very much influenced or confirmed Camus in his own,
especially in works like "Neither Victims Nor Executioners,"
"Reflections on the Guillotine" and *The Rebel*.

In newspapers and magazines and in conversation, Camus was
linked with a group of intellectuals including Jean-Paul Sartre, Simone
de Beauvoir and philosopher, Maurice Merleau-Ponty, who had also
worked in the Resistance. In the mid-1940s they were actively engaged
in social and political action, seeking to influence culture, society and
governance through the shaping of public ideas. Sartre, for example, was
a founder of the *Rassemblement Démocratique Révolutionnaire*, established
to give influence to intellectuals not allied with the Communists or any
other party, who wanted to see Europe as a non-aligned intermediary
between the United States and the Soviet Union. Camus participated in
some of its activities but never joined. In 1949, Sartre withdrew from the
Rassemblement when it seemed to him to be tainted by pro-American
tendencies, and made a strategic alliance with the Communists.
(Lottman, 441) Camus and his crowd spent their days writing and their
nights drinking, talking, seducing and even throwing punches at each
other in and around the nightspots of St. Germain-des-Pres. Camus
never appreciated being yoked politically or philosophically to Sartre
and rejected the label of existentialist when it was applied to his thought.
At the 1949 opening of his play *Les Justes*, Camus was standing, after the
performance, in the lobby with Sartre and Beauvoir. They were not the
friends they had been, but neither had they broken off with each other

yet. In *La force des chose*, Beauvoir relates that a woman approached Camus, and unaware of Sartre's presence said, "I like this better than *Les Mains sales*," a play by Sartre. Camus glanced at Sartre: "Two birds with one stone." (Lottman, 475)

Camus met Sartre in June 1943 right after he returned to Paris, now a successful author. At the premiere of Sartre's play *Les Mouche*, *The Flies*, Camus approached him and introduced himself. Soon after he met Sartre and Beauvoir at the Café de Flore, one of their customary hangouts, and they spoke at length. Sartre had just written *Huis Clos*, *No Exit*, on commission for an amateur actress, the wife of a pharmaceutical manufacturer, and they agreed that Camus would direct a production of it and play the male lead. Rehearsals began in Beauvoir's living room, but the project was suspended when the manufacturer's wife was arrested by the Gestapo for her connection with members of the Resistance. Sartre then decided to produce the play publicly with professional actors. Camus, Sartre, Beauvoir, Merleau-Ponty, Raymond Queneau, author of the surreal novel *Zazie dans le metro*, continued to see each other regularly, clandestinely listened to the BBC, discussed their ideas and ideals and imagined how they would influence the intellectual, political and cultural climate. They formed a floating salon of the intelligencia. They did the reading of *Le Désir attrapé par la queue*, in the living room of their friends, Louise and Michel Leiris. She was the daughter of the art dealer who represented Picasso; he was a writer, ethnologist and aficionado of bullfighting. Camus was the narrator, held a cane, which he thumped on the floor, as at the beginning of plays in the French theater, in order to indicate changes of scene, and read the stage directions. The living room was packed, included Picasso himself, Georges Braque, the painter, Georges Battaile, the erotic novelist, critic and philosopher, the actor-theater manager, Jean-Louis Barrault, with whom Camus would later stage several of his plays, the poet Henri Michaux and Casarès. After the reading, and after the audience had gone, the cast and their friends stayed, drinking and listening to jazz records. This event was the first of many, Leiris called them, "fiestas." (Lottman, 297–298)

In the matter of the Cold War, both Camus and Sartre began from the position that, as revolutionary leftist, they were not Stalinist. They stood outside the warring camps condemning both, adhering to the principles of individual liberty, freely chosen action and social justice. But after Sartre strategically allied himself with the communists, he and

Merleau-Ponty, although not endorsing them, did sometimes excuse Stalinist brutalities, arguing sophisticated versions of the principle that the end justifies the means. This was a position Camus had deplored in *The Myth of Sisyphus*, and despite his role in the war against German occupation, which was, for him, a battle against an immediate danger,[2] not a campaign to impose control, he still deplored it. Moreover, freedom and rebellion, which he saw as the defining characteristics of humanity, were stifled by ideology and brutality. The means of destruction, too, had become nuclear. His reading of Simone Weil and his friendship with Arthur Koestler, Soviet refugee author of *Darkness at Noon* and other books detailing the terrorism and brutality of Stalinism, reinforced his position.

At a party at the home of Boris Vians in 1947, shortly after Merleau-Ponty had written an article critical of Koestler's anti-Stalinism, Camus accused Merleau-Ponty of justifying the Moscow purge trials. (McCarthy, 87) Sartre defended Merleau-Ponty, and Camus left, according to Beauvoir's account, "visibly shaken, slamm[ing] the door," refusing to return when Sartre went after him. (Lottman, 405) His most forceful public statement of his position came in the essay "Neither Victims nor Executioners," where he argues against the ideologies and nationalisms dividing the world. He rejects brutality and the practice of regarding people as instruments of history, ideology or an abstraction like the State or a future good. He denies that it is possible to achieve a better world through power and dominance, or to make a world better for people tomorrow by making it worse for them today. The burden of Sisyphus, Camus had concluded, which requires devotion to the activity of the moment rather than to unachievable (putative) perfection is not a curse. It provides the basis in Camus's thought for the liberation of each person from the burden of being made to serve an interest abstracted from concern about actual individuals and their present experience. On a gut level, he was physically sickened by brutality. In "Reflections on the Guillotine," his famous tract against capital punishment, the foundation of his argument is an anecdote about his father. Before Camus was born, Lucien Camus had gone to see the public execution in Algeria of a man who had committed a brutal murder, and he favored executing him. But when he got home, Camus reports, pale faced, his father lay down on his bed and began vomiting.

His opposition to "revolutionary" violence and his "third camp" position supporting neither the United States nor the Soviet Union, derided by some as "moral," took Camus away from Sartre's group. Perhaps the first stage of his break with the ideological orthodoxy of revolutionary leftists—his final break would not come until the publication of *L'Homme revolté, The Rebel* in 1951—came in an interchange with Emanuel d'Astier after d'Astier wrote two articles in the pro-Soviet magazine *Action* attacking "Neither Victims nor Executioners" for Camus's condemnation of Soviet totalitarianism. When d'Astier challenged him, Camus pointed to the Soviet concentration and forced labor camps. D'Astier countered by suggesting Camus write an open letter to be published in American newspapers condemning U.S. complicity in the execution of political prisoners by the right-wing regime in Greece. After Camus responded by pointing out that he had addressed this issue during visits to Great Britain and the United States, he nevertheless agreed to write such a letter if d'Astier would condemn Soviet forced labor and concentration camps and demand the release of Spanish Republicans still incarcerated in the Soviet Union. D'Astier did not take up the challenge. What is most significant about this incident is that in his rebuttal Camus spoke of his role:

> My role [he wrote] is not to transform the world, nor man.... But it is, perhaps, to serve in my way the several values without which a world, even transformed, is not worth living.... If [Marxists] need [a conscience], who will give it to them if not these few men who, without separating themselves from history, conscious of their limits, seek to formulate as they can the misfortune and the hope of Europe. Solitaries! You will say with scorn. Perhaps, for the moment. (Lottman, 417–418)

It was a position which was often derided. Lionel Abel, the New York literary and social critic, wrote in the Partisan Review in 1949: "Camus's political writings, from what I have seen have become wordy, soft and vaguely noble." (Lottman, 452) Shortly after Camus's death, Sartre took several opportunities to show his contempt for a position favoring non-violence, with an oblique reference to Camus. "They look real fine," he wrote, "the nonviolent ones, neither victims nor executioners!" (Todd, 416)

As Camus indicated, there were a "few" among whom he could count himself. They were the group of artists and thinkers of an anarchist pacifist stripe. Among them was Dwight MacDonald, the essayist-activist editor of *Politics*, and the first to translate "Neither Victims nor Executioners" into English. Camus contributed to a little anarchist magazine *Témoins*, and was a member of the *Groupes de Liaison Internationale*, founded to support victims of totalitarianism, black or red. His vilification by former political and intellectual allies contributed to his withdrawal throughout the 1950s from public activism. Nevertheless he continued to work behind the scenes, writing letters in support of political prisoners and causes dear to him. In 1955, he testified on behalf of Maurice Laisant, a member of the anarchist group *Forces Libres de la Paix*, indicted for subversion for printing a poster opposing France's Indochina War in the anarchist paper *Le Libertaire*, edited by Camus's friend Maurice Joyeux. (Lottman, 543) In the last years of his life, he met with politicians of the Fourth Republic like Prime Minister Pierre Mendès-France and Presidents Guy Mollet and René Coty to discuss Algeria. He also met several times with de Gaulle himself regarding Algerian independence, and intervened successfully with him against the execution of Algerians fighting for separation from France, but Camus had little regard for him. Camus's biographer Oliver Todd reports that "when Camus suggested giving French citizenship to all Algerians," according to Francine Camus, "de Gaulle replied, 'Right, and we'll have fifty niggers in the Chamber of Deputies.'" (Todd, 387)

Political issues were not abstractions for Camus. They were matters of immediate human concern. The United States had actually used nuclear weapons against civilian populations. The Soviet Union had actually engineered the torture, imprisonment and murder of millions of people, and history had, during the early years of the decade, first unleashed the war that made him fatherless and then the undreamed of brutality of the fascist rampage. An issue especially close to Camus was Algeria where he was born, formed, had family and knew the people.

The German occupation made France a colonized nation, but the end of the war restored France to its status as a colonial power. The ongoing political catastrophe of the Fourth French Republic was decolonization. It defined the texture of French thought and politics. The most significant revolts against French rule occurred in Vietnam and Algeria. The French left Vietnam in 1954, after defeat in the battle of Dien Bien Phu, bequeathing their problems to the Americans. They remained enmeshed in Algeria longer, until the battle of Algiers in 1962.

Camus identified himself as an Algerian whose "native land [is] the French language." [Notebooks, 264] His attachment to Algeria was not colonial, and his French identification was not imperial. He did not desire Algeria to be a colony of France. He wanted it an independent part of a French confederation with equality and democracy for all its citizens, Europeans, Berbers and Arabs, with economic justice and the free exercise of all traditional cultures. He could not, however, support the violence of the Algerian revolutionaries or their rejection of European Algerians. He did not think in the excluding terms of nationalism, but in terms of people representing a variety of cultures inclusively joined together in and by a land. Consequently, he was traduced by some who were already upset by his condemnation of the Soviet Union, as being in favor of the imperial colonialism of France. It was a misperception that was painful to him that he stoically endured.

During this time, too, celebrity made demands on Camus. In 1946, he toured North America. A. J. Liebling, the American journalist who wrote about the press, interviewed him for *The New Yorker*, and the two became fast friends until Camus's death. In New York, too, he met Patricia Blake, who became and remained one of his lovers until his death. He stayed on Central Park West and 63rd Street in an apartment, lent to him by an admirer, and he and Patricia often walked through the park and stopped at the zoo. He liked Central Park, but the city's cavernous streets and towering skyscrapers made him uneasy. He found, however, a generosity of spirit in the people. When at the end of a talk he gave at Columbia University, from which the proceeds were to be used to help French orphans, Justin O'Brien, who translated *The Myth of Sisyphus* into English announced that the box office had been robbed, the audience paid again, and contributed even more.

In 1947, he published *The Plague* a novel which allegorized the German occupation of France and also abstracted from that occupation the absurdist problem of living meaningfully when an invincible evil, like Nazi disregard for life, or the undermining power of disease, like tuberculosis, obliterates meaning or hope. After the publication of *The*

Plague, Camus worked with Jean-Louis Barrault on a play with a similar theme, *L'Etat de siège*, *State of Siege*. The setting was moved from Oran in Algeria to Cadiz in Spain, the plague became a tyrannical leader, and the doctor who battled the plague became a student who rallied the people against the tyrant and chose death rather than halt his resistance.

In 1949, he crossed the Atlantic again, this time going to South America. The highlights of this trip for Camus came in Brazil, where his eagerness to see a soccer game delighted his hosts and endeared him to them, and in Chile, whose beauty reminded him of Algiers. In Argentina, where a production of *Le Malentendus* had been banned because of atheism, Camus refused to deliver a lecture in which he would condemn Peronist censorship of the press because it would have to be checked by the censors first. (*American Journals*, 131)

These travels were physically and emotionally taxing for him. Dislocation seemed to activate a melancholy that was as fundamental to him as his gregarious spirit and his devotion to spiritual and moral rectitude. His health, too, was fragile, and his accommodations were often trying. He suffered full-blown tuberculosis attacks and bouts of fever and lassitude, especially during the period spanning 1949 through 1951. By this time, streptomycin had replaced pneumothorax as the treatment for tuberculosis, and he suffered from side effects. During this period, too, his life with Francine got worse. Before the birth of their children, twins named Catherine and Jean, she seems to have been able to tolerate his liaisons with the other women he regularly saw, or at least to pretend they weren't happening, or to keep a deceiving hope that he would change. She also had an active life reading philosophy, teaching school, playing the piano and raising the children. She was often part of the party when Camus, Sartre, Koestler, Beauvoir and the others went to nightspots around Paris. The presence of spouses did not prevent affairs. Camus and Koestler's wife, Mamaine, became lovers and went to the south of France together. Koestler and Beauvoir had an affair. Sartre was famous for using his intelligence to attempt to intrigue women. In 1953, Francine's pain at Camus's indifference and her unreciprocated love became overwhelming. It was expressed in a depression that grew in severity into a full blown illness which included a suicide attempt and severe withdrawal, staring straight ahead and repeating the name Maria Casarès. Francine was hospitalized and subject to more than thirty electroshock treatments. Camus himself spoke of a struggle at this period against killing himself. He expressed guilt at what he called his Don Juanism, and "wondered" if his affairs weren't the cause of her illness. He spoke and wrote of his desire to be monastic. He saw the solution to his marital problems in a separation that never happened, although he often lived in his own rather than his family apartment. He believed in his freedom to love, even if it were unjust. "Love is injustice," he wrote in his *Notebook*, "but justice is not enough." (*Notebooks*, 250) Despite his bouts of regret, then, and despite an awareness of Francine's response to them, he continued his several attachments until his death.

Writing, too, was a torment and a struggle for Camus. In numerous letters addressed to a variety of recipients, men and women, lovers and friends, many to his wife, Camus complains about suffering and struggling as he composed his books or of agonizing during the periods when his work seemed blocked. His letters also show a serious intellectual if not sexual connection with Francine. He relied on her criticism of his works as he developed them. When he won the Nobel Prize in 1957, he asked Francine to come to Sweden with him. "Francine was there for the suffering, so it is normal that she should be there for the honors," he told Mi, the young Danish fashion model and soccer enthusiast he had begun seeing,

THE LAST DECADE

The paradoxes of his last decade weighed heavily on Camus. Winner of the prestigious Nobel Prize for Literature in November 1957, he would have preferred not to accept it, as he had declined many awards and honors. Simone Gallimard, who was at the award ceremony in Stockholm representing his publisher, noted he looked like he doubted he deserved it. Although he had published his last novel *The Fall* the year before and a collection of stories, *L'Exile et le royaume*, *Exile and the Kingdom*, in March he felt he was blocked, was struggling to write and felt himself isolated politically. The Nobel Prize could seem to signify an award for a career that had been finished, not one, as Camus repeatedly remarked was just coming into its maturity. (Lottman, 601) Roger Stéphane wrote venomously in *France-Observateur*:

> One wonders whether Camus is not on the decline and if, thinking they were honoring a young writer, the Swedish

Academy was not consecrating a precocious sclerosis.
(Lottman, 601)

But he was hardly barren in the fifties. Besides the stories and the novel,
he collected his essays, translated James Thurber's anti-war fable, *The
Last Flower*, issued *L'Eté, Summer*, a collection of lyrical essays, wrote
articles on Algeria for *L'Express* and adapted a number of plays for the
stage, plays he presented both in Paris and at the *Festival d'Art
Dramatique*. He had become the director of the festival, which was held
every summer at Angers in the city's thirteenth-century castle built by
Louis IX on the banks of the Maine River. It was a magnificent fortress
of a castle with towers, ramparts, a moat and drawbridge.

In his domestic life he was a man torn apart by an inability to unify
a life challenged by his contradictory dedication to family obligation and
personal freedom. Much, if not most of the time, he lived apart from
Francine, and he often lived with Maria Casarés in her apartment in
Paris. She performed at Angers in his adaptation of *Les Esprits*, a
sixteenth-century *commedia dell'arte* and in his adaptation of Pedro
Calderon's tragedy, *Devotion to the Cross*, which she co-translated from
the Spanish with Camus. In 1958, they traveled to Greece and spent two
weeks on Michel Gallimard's boat. It was in the summer of 1953, when
Casarès was working with Camus and his theater company in Angers
that Francine fell ill.

Camus's *Notebooks* are filled with fragments re-imagining and
recapitulating scenes from his marriage, arguments with his wife, and
analyses of himself and his situation:

> He shouted to her that this meant death for him and she did
> not consider herself touched. For with her lofty standards
> she considered it natural that he should die because he had
> failed. (*Notebooks*, 220)

Or:

> People insist on confusing marriage and love on the one
> hand, happiness and love on the other. But there is nothing
> in common. This is why it happens, the lack of love being
> more frequent than love, that some marriages are happy.
> (228)

Or:

> The moment I saw on her face an expression of pain, her will
> became mine: I was at my ease only when she was satisfied
> with me. (244)

Or:

> He told her that the love of men was like this, a will and not
> a grace, and that he had to conquer himself. She insisted to
> him that this was not love. (220)

Or:

> For him love was impossible. He was entitled only to lies and
> adultery. (258)

Or:

> Those two wretched creatures who were known solely to
> each other on earth, who were the only ones capable of doing
> each other justice, of understanding and consoling each
> other, seemed two irreconcilable enemies, bent on tearing
> each other apart. (244)

In his public life he was a man lacerated by the pain of the rejection
and attack he had endured by remaining loyal to his vision of intellectual
honesty and human complexity. He was firm in his opposition to
violence in the service of justice in general and specifically with regard
to the FLN's (the Algerian National Liberation Front's) program of
random bombings in public places. After being vilified and cast off by
Sartre and his group for "Neither Victims nor Executioners" and then
for *The Rebel*, being awarded the Nobel Prize brought as much scorn
upon him as praise, from the right as well as from the left. Contrary to
the doctrinaire leftists who branded Camus crypto-colonialist, rightists
considered him dangerously radical, especially because of his opposition
to French domination of Algeria and because he was friendly with some
of the rebels and often spoke up in their defense. His position on Algeria
became an issue at the Nobel Prize celebrations, too. Shortly before
going to Stockholm, Camus had written to the defense attorney for Ben
Saddok—an Algerian Moslem on trial for killing a Moslem who did not

support the FLN—that he would intervene on his behalf if the letter he wrote to the court would not be made public, nor even his act of intervention.

> I have been refusing for the past two years [he wrote] and I shall continue to refuse until I see the possibility of useful action, any public manifestation susceptible of being exploited politically to add to the misfortune of my country. In particular, I wish in no case to give a good conscience, by statements bearing no personal risk to me, to the stupid fanatic who in Algeria might fire into a crowd where my mother and all my loved ones would be. (Lottman, 612)

In Stockholm, during an open question and answer session, a young Algerian Moslem challenged Camus to explain why he readily spoke up against Soviet domination in Eastern Europe, but was silent regarding Algeria, and embellished his question with a harangue against Camus. Shaken, Camus spoke personally, first saying, "I have never spoken to an Arab or to one of your militants as you have just spoken to me in public.... let me finish my sentences because often sentences take on their full meaning only at the end." (Lottman, 617) Camus then did address the substance of the question, pointing out that he defended Moslems while a journalist in Algeria, supported a free, democratic regime, and was reluctant to speak out now after having seen how the pronouncements of intellectuals often made the situation worse. He concluded saying publicly what he had written to Saddok's lawyer:

> I must ... denounce a terrorism which is exercised blindly, in the streets of Algiers for example, and which some day could strike my mother or my family. I believe in justice, but I shall defend my mother above justice. (Lottman, 618)

Just as he was torn between Europe and Africa, his wife and his lovers, his success as a writer and his sense of despair at the impotence of his work, he also was torn between pleasure and duty, as he makes clear in his *Notebooks*: "My chief occupation, despite appearances has always been love.... I have a romantic soul and have always had considerable trouble interesting it in something else." (*Notebooks*, 235)

"There is in me an anarchy, a frightful disorder. Creating costs me a thousand deaths, for it involves an order and my whole being rebels against order." (238)

French intellectuals after the Second World War found themselves neatly divided into left and right camps. Although not all leftists were communists, it was *de rigueur* for communists and non-communist leftists to be anti-anti-communist, de-emphasizing the barbarities of Stalinism for the sake, as they saw it, of preserving revolutionary hope. Anti-communism was therefore seen as a rightist position, one tactic in a general campaign to subvert revolutionary possibility by devotees of capitalism who felt no discomfort at its iniquities. Camus took his place as an anti-communist in the 1950s without becoming a rightist, staunch in his refusal to be intimidated by categories, asserting that "If, finally, truth seemed to me on the right, I would be there." (Lottman, 504) But it didn't appear to be there for him. For him it appeared as a vision of individuals *as* individuals living together cooperatively without coercion and violence, realizing differences and confederating around their humanity and in opposition to its brutalization by totalitarian forces or the irrationality of nature. In the early 1950s, even as he was denouncing Stalinism, or the Soviet invasion of Hungary, he was also publicly opposing Franco's fascism in Spain. He spoke at rallies to prevent the execution of Spanish political prisoners, and withdrew as a consultant to the United Nations Educational Social and Cultural Oraganization (UNESCO) when it allowed the Franco regime to be a member. (Lottman, 502)

The notorious catalytic event of the early 1950s that created the rupture between Camus and Sartre—isolating Camus from the fellowship he had enjoyed when he had embodied the romantic, tough intellectual of bohemian Paris, writing, editing *Combat*, choosing books for publication at Gallimard by day and doing Paris by night in the midst of a band of celebrated friends, the collar of his trench coat up and a cigarette hanging from his mouth—was the publication of *The Rebel* in October 1951.

Camus had been formulating the ideas he put forward in *The Rebel* throughout the 1940s. The book is a response to the brutality of the Nazi regime, the terror and torture of Soviet Stalinism, and the worldwide threat of nuclear war that lay at the root of the Cold War. *The Rebel* is a corollary to *The Myth of Sisyphus*. That book concerned each person's relation to himself, indicated by the dominant question of suicide. The focus of *The Rebel* is the relation of the individual to other individuals. Its fundamental question is murder. Just as Camus rejected suicide as a way to respond to a sense of individual meaninglessness, so he rejected murder as a vehicle for justice, or a way to deal with differences between people or conflicts between nations. In *The Rebel*, Camus mapped out a position that was radically independent. Rebellion was not beholden to the ideology of communism, either as it was practiced, nor in a "pure" form either. Camus argued that the Marxist adaptation of the Hegelian teleological model of history—that history was going somewhere, and mankind had to follow, or else!—made the system it generated inevitably totalitarian because ends perforce dominated means. *The Rebel* argued for the value of the immediate possibility of the living present, against sacrificing the present in the name of the future. Philosophically and politically, Camus saw rebellion as the way out of the meaningless irrationality of the Absurd. His heroic emblem had metamorphosed from Sisyphus to Prometheus.

In the August 1951 issue, Sartre had published a chapter on Nietzsche from *The Rebel* in *Les Temps Modernes*. In May 1952, *Les Temps Moderne* printed a review of *The Rebel* which Sartre had chosen Francis Jeanson to write. Jeanson was a young disciple who had recently written a book about him. He fought with the Free French in North Africa during the Second World War. From 1957 to 1962 he was underground; from Italy he worked with the FLN against the French. (Lottman, 500) Camus's condemnation of Cold War partisanship and political violence, his rejection of the ineluctability of history and his search for moral rectitude and commitment to the present rankled the Sartrists. In his more than twenty page review of *L'Homme Revolté*, Jeanson wrote:

> Is Camus's hope really to halt the movement of the world by refusing every endeavor in the world? He blames the Stalinists ... for being totally captive of history; but they are not more so than he is, they are only captive in another way.... To the extent that [Camus wants revolt] to influence the movement of the world it must enter into the game, insert itself into the historical context, find its objectives there, its adversaries.... (Lottman, 502)

He denigrated Camus's thought by calling it "infinitely flexible and malleable, apt to acquire many different forms ... vague humanism with just a touch of anarchism." Moreover, he asserted, Camus "denied any role at all to historical and economic elements in the birth of revolutions." (Todd, 307)

Camus was pained by what he saw as a betrayal of friendship and a pseudo-proletarian posturing on the part of people comfortably bourgeois, willing to subordinate persons to policies. He responded to Jeanson's review with a letter. Sartre printed it and his own *ad hominem* response: "I don't reproach you," he wrote with a Ciceronian flourish, referring to the style of Camus's letter, "for its pomp, since that comes naturally to you, but for the smoothness with which you handle your indignation. Our friendship," Sartre wrote:

> was not an easy one, but I shall miss it.... A mixture of somber self-conceit and of vulnerability has always discouraged anyone from telling you whole truths. The result is that you have become the victim of bleak immoderation which masks your internal difficulties.... What if your book simply shows your philosophical incompetence? What if it is made up of secondhand knowledge, hastily collected?.... And if your reasoning is inaccurate? And if your thoughts are vague and banal? ... At least I have this in common with Hegel, that you haven't read either one of us.... I don't dare advise you go back to *Being and Nothingness* [Sartre's book of Existential philosophy], since reading it would be needlessly difficult for you. You hate difficulties of thought and you hastily decree that there is nothing to understand, in order to avoid reproaches of not having understood things, before they develop. (Lottman, 504; Todd, 309)

Sartre also did address substantive aspects of Camus's work, conceding, regarding Soviet forced labor camps:

> ... yes, Camus, I find these camps just as unacceptable as you do. But I find equally unacceptable the use that the so-called bourgeois press makes of them every day.... If we apply your principles, the Vietminh [the group opposed to French

colonial occupation in Vietnam, led by Ho Chi Minh, which
would become the government of North Vietnam and then,
in 1975, of the reunified country] are colonized and
therefore slaves, but because they are communists they are
also tyrants at the same time. (Todd, 309)

Sartre's contention that printing propaganda can be equivalent to
imprisoning, torturing and killing people in forced labor camps, as was
the Soviet practice, is surely exaggerated. It is also off the mark when
used as a reproach to Camus who so often condemned the western bloc
with the observation that its existence is the only thing that could be
used as an argument for the communists. Camus was even-handed. He
refused to remain a member of the *Société Européen de Culture* because its
members failed to condemn Soviet forced labor camps, or to participate
in Moscow sponsored "peace conferences." He similarly refused to
participate in the activities or sign the manifestos of the Congress for
Cultural Freedom, a front for the American CIA. Despite his friendship
with Arthur Koestler or his agreement regarding Soviet tyranny, he did
not join Koestler in Cold War partisanship for the United States. He
was unaware that *Encounter* and *Preuve*, magazines for which he
occasionally wrote, were funded by the CIA. He declined Henry
Kissenger's repeated requests to contribute to the international journal,
Confluence, which Kissenger edited at Harvard. (Lottman, 433) At the
time of this conflict, too, Camus refused to publish defenses of his book
or his stand or attacks on his critics or polemics against Stalinism in the
rightist journals which offered him space. In his comment about the
Vietminh, Sartre is most likely trying to demonstrate the absurdity of
Camus's position arguing that it leads to contradiction. That it is not a
contradiction is precisely what Camus is asserting. Because of a wealth
of circumstances, people can be both victims and executioners, and, he
pleads, must strive to become neither.

   Camus made no further response, but positions had been defined,
and it was only after Camus's death that Sartre reconciled with him,
writing, "We were on bad terms, he and I, but bad terms mean nothing,
even if we'd have never met again, it's just another way of living
together." (Todd, 415) The irony is that this sentence recalls the nub of
their difference: Sartre's ability to abstract from immediacy and to value
an idea above a person. Sartre proceeded then to recognize as virtues in
Camus what he had taken as shortcomings in 1952:

He represented in this century, and against History, the
present-day heir of that long line of moralists whose work
constitute what is perhaps most original in French letters.
His stubborn humanism, strict and pure, austere and sensual,
delivered uncertain combat against the massive and
deformed events of the day. But inversely, by the
unexpectedness of his refusals, he reaffirmed, at the heart of
our era, against the Machiavelians, against the golden calf of
realism, the existence of the moral act. (Lottman, 673)

Not everyone condemned *The Rebel* when it appeared or
considered it a move towards conservatism. Hanna Arendt, German
Jewish refugee philosopher, respected for her study *On Totalitarianism*,
wrote to Camus from the United States expressing how much she liked
the book. Contradicting Camus's gloomy assessment that despite the
book's commercial success, *The Rebel* "is a book that sells but isn't read,"
(Todd, 306) it became a guiding text. In the United States it helped many
of the young on college and high school campuses to formulate their
challenge to the complacency and the values which had defined the
conformity culture of the 1950s. In France, it was considered by some to
have been one of the works that strongly influenced the shape and
definition of the vision and the values that formed the workers and the
students who led the revolt of May 1968.

The battering of spirit that Camus suffered in the 1950s serves as
the basis for some of the stories in *Exile and the Kingdom* and for his last
complete novel, *La Chute, The Fall*. In "Jonas" Camus follows the
withdrawal into isolation of an artist first celebrated for his work. *The
Fall* is written as a monologue from the underground. It is delivered by
a once renowned lawyer who is a guilty refugee from the grace he once
enjoyed after he has seen through the inauthenticity of his own and
other people's virtue and sounded the depth of his own emptiness—an
emptiness he discovered one night as he passed a woman on a bridge
who threw herself into the Seine, and he did not stop to save her. *The
Fall* reflects the bitterness of his break with Sartre, mockery of himself
and those who vilified him, and his guilt with regard to Francine.

Undoubtedly the pain of his personal and public trials was greatly
increased by the fact that throughout the 1950s Camus remained a
terribly sick man. One of the effects of tuberculosis was that he was

sometimes overcome by choking and by the feeling that he was suffocating. In one instance, he was overcome on the street, managed to have a passerby get him a cab, and was rushed to his doctor's office where oxygen was administered. His secretary often had to walk home with him, and a specialist explained that he was half asphyxiated and that his brain was not getting enough oxygen. The breathing exercises he learned to do did not help very much. (Lottman, 621) This physical distress as much as any emotional bitterness can well account for his complaint of "amnesia" to the actress, Catherine Sellers, one of his lovers, in 1957. To Francine, the same year, he wrote: "I've never known such a state as I find myself in now, with no memories or even feelings, and deeply humiliated no longer to feel the heart inside me...." (Todd, 366) To his friend Roger Quillot he confided:

> I've just gone through a long and bad period of depression complicated by respiratory difficulties, and during which I wasn't able to work. Just recently I've begun to catch my breath, which is the right word for it. (Lottman, 625)

The last years of his life, were full of artistic, intellectual, personal and political frustration. He remarked to the television producer, Pierre Cardinal, who was interviewing him, and with whom he planned to make a television film of *La Chute* in which he, Camus, would play the novel's narrator "I always have the impression that I have to ask forgiveness for something." (Lottman, 649–650) This may be an example of his dry irony, aimed less at himself than at the battery of those who faulted his stands. Writing came hard to him. Theater was his refuge. His adaptation of William Faulkner's *Requiem for a Nun* was a success in Paris. He also fashioned a drama from Doestoevsky's sprawling novel *The Possessed*, again returning to the problem of violence in the service of revolution or justice. He did not, however, withdraw from social involvement, but his engagement became more complex and inward:

> When two of our brothers engage in a fight without mercy, it is criminal madness to excite one or the other of them. Between wisdom reduced to silence and madness which shouts itself hoarse, I prefer the virtues of silence. Yes, when speech manages to dispose without remorse of the existence

of others, to remain silent is not a negative attitude. (Lottman, 626)

In March 1958, two months before de Gaulle returned to power, he consulted with Camus regarding his position on Algeria. Many had faith that de Gaulle could solve the Algerian problem, but was playing his cards close to his vest, allowing each faction to believe he favored them. Camus, apparently, was asked to join de Gaulle's government in a cultural office, but declined. He also declined to represent the government on a government appointed panel of Nobel laureates investigating charges of French torture in Algeria. (Lottman, 625, 629, 631)

Winning the Nobel Prize brought Camus the equivalent of 45,000 dollars. He gave a little of it to charity, and with the rest he bought a house in Lourmarin in the south of France. He had several reasons for the purchase. It was a place for his family to live, a place for him to write, a place removed from the uncongenial world of Paris, a place near his good friend, the poet, René Char. He would divide his time between Lourmarin and Paris. He could spend much of the winter there, and Francine would be in Paris where she taught.

On January 3, 1960, Camus was planning to take the train back to Paris from Lourmarin, but changed his mind at the last minute—there was a railroad ticket found in his wallet—allowing himself to be persuaded to drive back with his friends Michel and Janine Gallimard. Michel drove. The two men were sitting in the front talking. Michel was not speeding, the roads were wet, he lost control of the car, hit a tree, and Camus was dead instantly. Michel Gallimard died a week later. Camus's briefcase was found at the scene of the accident. Among its contents was an eighty thousand word manuscript he had begun work on, the draft of a novel, *Le premiere homme*, which was to be his *Bildugsroman*. Edited by his daughter Catherine from his closely written first draft, it was published in 1995.

His death made headlines round the world. He was buried in the cemetery at Lourmarin, without a church service. In attendance were his wife, Francine, Gaston Gallimard and his wife, Gabriel Audisio, representing the *Société des Gens des Lettres*, and René Char. The bell tolling for him tolled not from a church steeple but, from Lourmarin's village clock tower. The mound of his grave is marked by an aged stone bearing his name and dates. It is covered by a thick growth of rosemary.

NOTES

1. http://members.bellatlantic.net/~samg2/freedom.html [accessed 1/29/03]

2. See Lottman, 624. Suzanne Angley, Camus's secretary at Gallimard reports that in response to an Algerian interlocutor's challenge "demanding to know why Camus didn't join the Moslem's liberation movement ... [reminding] him that he had accepted [violence and murder] during the Nazi occupation [of France], Camus [later told her] 'It's true that I wasn't shocked by resistance to the Nazis because I was French and my country was occupied.'"

WORK CITED

Bree, Germaine. *Camus.* New York: Harbinger Books, Harcourt, Brace & World, Inc., 1964.

Camus, Albert. *American Journals.* Translated by Hugh Levick (New York: Paragon House Publishers, 1987).

———— *Notebooks, 1942–1951.* New York: Alfred A. Knopf, 1965.

Lottman, Herbert R. *Albert Camus: A Biography.* Garden City, NY: Doubleday & Company, Inc., 1970.

McCarthy, Patrick. *Camus.* New York: Random House, 1982.

Oxenhandler, Neal. "Success Story," in *Looking for Heroes in Postwar France: Albert Camus, Max Jacob, Simone Weil.* Hanover, NH and London: Dartmouth College/University Press of New England, 1996.

Todd, Olivier. Albert Camus: A Life. Translated by Benjamin Ivry. New York: Knopf, 1997.

http://members.bellatlantic.net/~samg2/freedom.html [accessed 1/7/03]

JENN McKEE

Exile, Revolt, and Redemption:
The Writings of Albert Camus

INTRODUCTION

Although Albert Camus wrote a broad range of work—including short stories, plays, essays, philosophical tracts, and a handful of novels—during his relatively short career, it is profoundly apropos that the single work for which he is most famous is entitled *The Stranger*. Meursault, that novel's famous main character, exists with a sense of the world and a morality that sets him apart from human society at large. Similarly, in his notebooks, Camus often hinted at an overriding sense of always being an outsider in the world, no matter his location or circumstances; once, for instance, he wrote, "It is constantly my lot to remain apart," though he was well-known for his charm, particularly his success with women; and, as an impoverished Frenchman who was born in colonized Algeria, he noted, "Yes, I have a native land: the French language," thus emphasizing the sense of displacement felt by a man who belonged in neither the rich, colonialist French society of Algeria[1], nor the native, poor, Moslem population.

In addition, late in Camus's life, his politics and personal beliefs, particularly regarding Communism and the struggle within Algeria, set him diametrically apart from the dominant members of Paris intelligentsia, including the existentialist peer with whom he's most often paired (and with whom he'd previously shared a friendship): Jean-Paul Sartre. But despite the fact that many critics, past and present, view

Camus as an intellectual "lightweight" among the existentialists[2]—producing contradiction-riddled philosophic tracts that presented the ideas of others with only a vague, oversimplified understanding of their work, and that touted a kind of "can't we all just get along" mantra that seemed unrealistic, bourgeois, and pithy to his peers—few twentieth century writers captured the imagination and interest of so many. Sartre may well have been Camus's intellectual superior, but Camus provided readers with something far more strangely, electrifyingly intimate: a naked demonstration of a man struggling doggedly to determine his literal and figurative place in the world.

To this end, an unnerving contradiction persists in much of Camus's work: it is personal—in that we learn in great detail what likely kept Camus awake at night—but wholly impersonal as well, since, until the very end of his career, his personal experiences stayed outside the realm of his writing. Even in Camus's own notebooks, translator/critic Phillip Thody's introduction notes that the journals kept between 1935 and 1942 "did not contain any open reference either to his first or to his second marriage, and provided no details about his membership in the Communist Party or his work as a journalist on *Alger-Républicain*" (Thody, *iv*).[3] Scholar Paul de Man also noticed Camus's remoteness from his own journals: "Camus deliberately tore himself away from his natural inclinations and forced upon himself a number of alien concerns. As a result, the *Notebooks* reflect an increasing feeling of estrangement and solitude. One feels an almost obsessive commitment to work, a rejection of any moment of private experience as self-indulgence" (21).

However, in spite of Camus's fierce efforts to keep his work and personal life separate, the sudden and early end of his life—a car accident in France in 1960, when Camus was only forty-six—came shortly after a seemingly drastic change in his perspective; for inside that car was a working draft of his novel, *The First Man*, the most blatantly personal work he wrote. From this, as well as information provided by biographers Olivier Todd and Herbert R. Lottman, we learn about the major events of Camus's life, specifically those that left permanent scars and echoed throughout his writings: his widowed mother's illiteracy, partial deafness, and near silence; his family's extreme poverty in Algeria; his diagnosis, at age seventeen, of tuberculosis, which afflicted him on and off throughout his life[4]; his life in Nazi-occupied France during World War II; and, finally, his quarrel and break with Parisian Leftist intellectuals after the publication of *The Rebel*, which worked in part to critique and condemn communism. Thus, if we interpret these turning points as Camus's raw material, we notice experience after experience that likely made the writer feel the full weight of his solitude, in ways large and small.

Not surprisingly, critics have long taken note of, and examined, the different ways in which emotional and physical separation manifests itself in Camus's texts. But as critic Germaine Bree noted, Camus's readers and critics "shared his concern with the ambient problems, political, ethical, or philosophical," and so "the terrain covered by critical studies of Camus's work is consequently very broad, and often reflects the strains and stresses of a particular historical moment" (Bree, 2).

BETWIXT AND BETWEEN AND NUPTIALS

In 1937, Camus was a twenty-three-year-old journalist for the newspaper *Alger-Républicain* and already divorced from his troubled, drug-addicted first wife, Simone Hié. His first collection of lyrical essays, *Betwixt and Between* (sometimes translated as *The Wrong Side and the Right Side*) was published that year, while *Nuptials* was published two years later. The essays in both books largely reflected Camus's love of Algeria, with long, winding, poetic sentences and sensuous descriptions of the landscape and its people. Hellenist and pantheistic elements thus pervade the essays, which is no surprise, given Camus's fixation on Greek thought and culture.

In this vein, critics have often cited the eroticization of nature in these collections, which re-appears in works throughout Camus's career. For instance, in "Nuptials at Tipasa," Camus writes (after referencing, in passing, the myth of Demeter): "Yet even here, I know that I shall never come close enough to the world. I must be naked and dive into the sea, still scented with the perfumes of the earth, wash them off in the sea, and consummate with my flesh the embrace for which sun and sea, lips to lips, have so long been sighing ... On the beach, I flop down on the sand, yield to the world, feel the weight of flesh and bones, again dazed with sunlight, occasionally glancing at my arms where the water slides off and patches of salt and soft blond hair appear on my skin. Here I understand what is meant by glory: the right to love without limits ... To clasp a woman's body is also to hold in one's arms this strange joy that descends from sky to sea. In a moment ... I shall know, appearances to the contrary, that I am fulfilling a truth which is the sun's and which will also be my death's." Similar to this moment, Meursault, in *The Stranger*, goes swimming with Martha, his soon-to-be lover, and it is in the sea that their affair begins. Also, a famous moment in *The Plague* features Rieux, the main character, breaking away from the months-long oppression of his town's quarantine by going for a swim. He and his friend Tarrou go into the off-limits waters near the city of Oran, and a sense of happy fulfillment washes over them. Critics have noted that this moment intimately bonds the two men together and provides a sense of release for both characters (as well as Camus's readers).

In this way, we see Algeria's landscape and climate informing much of Camus's work, thematically and symbolically. In addition to presenting water as an element of renewal, connection, freedom, and re-birth, Camus also often refers to the sun as an oppressive, intolerant, violent force. For instance, in *The Stranger*, Camus describes the sun, in the critical murder scene, as a sort of accomplice—if not the main impetus—to Meursault in the shooting of the Arab on the beach, as critics like Roger Quilliot and John Erickson have noted. Neither the employment of water or of the sun as symbols, of course, is original in any way, but some critics, like S. Beynon John, have noted how this conventional use of symbols places Camus among neo-Romanticists, and because of Camus's intensely personal, sensual use of these familiar symbols, "they remain free of the deliberate and rather artificial air they sometimes wear" ("Image and Symbol" 144).

In addition to introducing symbols, Camus's early work also briefly hinted at the heartbreak he felt at the inaccessibility of his nearly mute mother. Though the full picture isn't made clear until the publication of *The First Man*, thirty-four years after Camus's death, we do get, in the essay "Between Yes and No," a small window through which to view Camus's private agony. Speaking of "the child," rather than "I"—and thus emphasizing distance even from himself—Camus wrote, "He feels sorry for his mother; is this the same as loving her? She has never hugged or kissed him, for she wouldn't know how. He stands a long time watching her. Feeling separate from her, he becomes conscious of her suffering. She does not hear him, for she is deaf." This forecasts not only an image that will come back in subsequent works, but also seems to shape Camus's repeated failure to include female characters of any complexity or significance in his prose.

Finally, the early essays also hinted at where he would progress next intellectually. Regarding death, he wrote, in "The Wind at Djemila," "I do not want to believe that death is the gateway to another life. For me, it is a closed door. I do not say ... I have too much youth in me to be able to speak of death. But it seems to me that if I had to speak of it, I would find the right word here between horror and silence to express the conscious certainty of a death without hope." And later, in "The Desert," Camus wrote: "And what more legitimate harmony can unite a man with life than the dual consciousness of his longing to endure and his awareness of death? ... [this landscape] took me out of myself in the deepest sense of the word. It assured me that but for my love and the wondrous cry of these stones, there was no meaning in anything. The world is beautiful, and outside it there is no salvation." Thus, in early passages such as these, we perhaps see Camus's first grapplings with existentialism and the notion of the absurd, concepts that would absorb his thoughts and pervade his writing for the next several years.

CAMUS'S PRACTICE NOVEL: A HAPPY DEATH

Before discussing and examining Camus's absurd cycle, however, I should note that while Camus wrote and published the lyrical essays in *Betwixt and Between* and *Nuptials*, he also struggled with his first attempted novel, *A Happy Death*, which acted as a kind of writing warm-up for Camus's *The Stranger*. First published posthumously in 1972, *A Happy Death* shows Camus asking, through the actions of Patrice Mersault (a clear forerunner of *The Stranger*'s narrator), whether one can possibly meet death feeling content with how he lived his life. In this case, Mersault, living and working as a clerk in Algeria, decides that a lack of money keeps him from the freedom he needs to live and be fulfilled, so he kills a rich, paralyzed man named Zagreus.[5] Mersault soon quits his job as a clerk, travels, stays in a house with three women who are friends, leaves them and soon marries, then dies of an illness that began with a chill on the same night of the murder. In the end, Mersault does indeed die happy, telling readers, "And all those who had not made the gestures necessary to live their lives, all those who feared and exalted impotence—they were afraid of death because of the sanction it gave to a life in which they had not been involved. They had not lived enough, never having lived at all ... what did it matter if he existed for two or for twenty years? Happiness was the fact that he had existed." Again, this kind of perspective on death, life, and priorities pointed Camus in the direction of his next work, which would catapult him, overnight, into the spotlight.

THE ABSURD CYCLE

> I do believe at least that man's awareness of his destiny has never ceased to advance. We have not overcome our condition, and yet we know it is better. We know that we live in contradiction, but we also know that we must refuse this contradiction and do what is needed to reduce it.
>
> —"The Almond Trees," 1940

Although Camus had published essays and gained some recognition from his work as a journalist in Algeria, it wasn't until 1942—two years after he married Francine Faure in Oran and then moved by himself to Paris—that the publication of both *The Stranger* and his philosophical work *The Myth of Sisyphus* brought him fame. These works, along with the plays, *Caligula* and *The Misunderstanding*, formed what Camus originally planned, according to his journal, as his "absurd" cycle. "Absurd," however, is a term that must be clearly defined in order to understand Camus's ideas.

Camus believed there was no God, and he struggled with the consequences of that premise—i.e., if there's no afterlife, and life is meaningless, is it worth living? The first line of *The Myth of Sisyphus* cuts right to this point, stating, "There is but one truly serious philosophical problem, and that is suicide." What strikes Camus as absurd is mankind's perpetual hope for an afterlife, or immortality, in spite of man's certain knowledge that death is inevitable. Near the end of his essay, Camus points to Sisyphus as the ultimate Absurd hero, in that the mythical Greek figure keeps pushing the rock uphill again and again, though its rolling back down is a foregone conclusion, and Sisyphus himself is aware of this never-changing consequence and his life's fate. Camus concentrates most on that instant before Sisyphus heads back down the hill, and the last line of the essay claims that, "One must imagine Sisyphus happy." Thus, Camus champions the person who is wholly aware of his/her absurd plight, but who nonetheless chooses not only to live, but to seek out happiness and embrace life, all of it, good and bad.

The Stranger aligns itself with this idea, focusing on an Algerian Frenchman, Meursault, who ambivalently attends his mother's funeral, has a love affair, shoots and kills a man (who had stabbed Meursault's friend) on the beach, and finds himself standing trial, more for not properly mourning his mother—thus not acting in accordance to society's norms and laws—rather than for the murder itself. Critics have paid much attention to the style Camus adopts in the novel, which is starkly different from everything else he wrote—short, simple sentences that underline the utter detachment of the narrator from those around him, his world, and the reader. Roland Barthes called the style "white writing," describing it as "a colourless writing, freed from all bondage to a pre-ordained state of language" and "a style of absence that is almost an ideal absence of style." The cold detachment of the book's first sentences, in fact, jars readers profoundly: "Mother died today. Or, maybe, yesterday; I can't be sure. The telegram from the Home says: YOUR MOTHER PASSED AWAY. FUNERAL TOMORROW. DEEP SYMPATHY. Which leaves the matter doubtful; it could have been yesterday." This opening indicates immediately that the world and perspective we are entering is not emotionally familiar; it is that of a stranger, indeed.

Other critics have focused on how native Algerians—or "Arabs"—are depicted in the novel, and in Camus's work in general. Some have discussed how Camus's unique position allowed him access to the truths of a culture different from his own, but others, including John Erickson, reject this idea, stating that Camus merely revealed a "representation" of the North African Arab culture "from a position of exteriority." As evidence, Erickson points out that although nearly all of Camus's works are set in Algeria, few to no Moslem characters appear, and almost none are particularly positive and/or three dimensional portrayals; thus, in spite of Camus's strident, insistent position of neutrality on the Algeria question later in his life, Erickson works to prove Camus's colonialist leanings, showing that his aesthetic presentation belied his true politics.

Still other critics deal with the question of judgment and morality that looms large in *The Stranger*. Critic René Girard equates Camus's depiction of Meursault to that of a child:

If the child is left alone, his solitude quickly becomes
unbearable but pride prevents him from returning meekly to
the family circle. What can he do, then, to re-establish
contact with the outside world? He must commit an action
that will force the attention of the adults but that will not be
interpreted as abject surrender, a *punishable* action, of course
(Girard, 100).

Camus thus leads readers to feel that Meursault, though technically a
murderer, is the victim, and that the bases for his sentencing are out of
sync with reality, and in this way, Camus appears to condemn judgment
of any kind, claiming that no one in a Godless world has the authority to
do so. All actions are thus rendered equal importance and impact:
washing hands, eating an apple, shooting a man. For without religion
and God, the former basis of our morality, what do our actions mean,
after all?

Camus's depiction of a meaningless, Godless universe quickly
situated him as a peer of other existentialist writers (though Camus
resisted this label throughout his career), such as Jean-Paul Sartre. It also
caused him to be perpetually associated with the notion of the absurd
throughout his career, which became a source of frustration for him—
for although his works on the absurd made him famous, they were
limited to the individual's understanding of himself, his circumstances,
and his own death. Many scholars recognized, however, that Camus
evolved from the notion of the absurd to the next logical questions—
how does that inevitably doomed individual conduct him/herself within
a community, or society? Do we agree on a morality in the absence of
God, and if so, on what basis?—but some, much to Camus's chagrin,
applied his first ideas every successive work.

And while *Myth* and *The Stranger* enjoyed success, Camus still
struggled with a play titled *Caligula*, which he started in 1938 but kept
re-writing, never quite satisfied. He also wrote a play titled *The
Misunderstanding* during this time, and although *Caligula* is a better fit in
Camus's absurd cycle, most critics focus on both plays when discussing
this grouping.

The Misunderstanding, first performed in 1944, tells the expanded,
slightly altered story that first appeared, in abbreviated form, in *The
Stranger*. When Meursault is in prison, he reads a scrap of newspaper

about a man who returns to his family after many years, doesn't identify himself, and ends up being killed by them for his money. In *The Misunderstanding*, Jan is the son who returns after becoming rich, looking to help his mother and sister. Martha is his sister who, along with her mother, dreams of leaving Czechoslovakia for a warm coast, to live on a beach, so she could always feel the sun that "burns out people's souls and gives them bodies that shine like gold but are quite hollow, there's nothing left inside," a place where "the sun kills every question" (demonstrating again Camus's repeated thematic use of this symbol).

Martha and her mother run a hotel, where they kill and rob their rare clients, and from the outset, the audience sees and knows precisely what will happen. Camus, with this play and others, tries hard to create a modern Greek tragedy, which, for him, was a lifelong goal. But many critics condemn this play, among others written by Camus, as unproducable—a play that should be read, not performed. Scholars fault Camus both for being too self-conscious about promoting his philosophical ideas, thus sacrificing the story, as well as writing characters that have little to no psychological complexity or depth.

Also, *The Misunderstanding*, in spite of its timing, seemed only moderately aligned with *Myth* and *The Stranger*. Martha and her mother *do* act on their own impulses, without a larger, Judeo-Christian-based morality guiding their behavior; however, the mother feels a sense of guilt upon learning the truth, thus judging herself, and there appears to be no hint of how happiness in life can be sought and temporarily achieved in the face of absurdity. The very dream that guides the women's actions—living near a beach—is not one of fulfillment, but rather, one of reaching a setting that sucks out souls, leaving bodies hollow. In other works, Camus's vision involves some moments of joy, even while confronting man's contradictions head-on; for although Camus thought it foolish to hope for an afterlife, he did not find the search for happiness in life foolish in the least.

Caligula, which wasn't produced until 1945, after the end of the Nazi occupation in France, features the infamous Roman emperor, depressed by his lover/sister's death. Consequently, he flaunts the accepted rules and conventions of his society. He kills people with little or no cause, sleeps with the wives of friends, demands exorbitant sums from his already-taxed citizens, and dresses as Venus, performing on stage in drag.

Caligula easily fulfills the criteria of the absurd man: in facing the death of his sister, he contends with death's inevitability, as well as the seeming meaninglessness of life. Of course, the significance of someone in Caligula's position of power having this realization is that his decisions and random actions have much more far-reaching consequences. The original audiences of 1945, obviously, saw the embodiment of Hitler on stage as Caligula, and E. Freeman, the foremost critical voice on Camus's plays, notes that the play also worked to forecast the "revolt cycle" that would follow in Camus's work, with Caligula embodying the wrong kind of revolt—that which costs others' lives without sacrifice, and goes to absolutist extremes. Freeman also noted that the all-important alternative—revolt with limits—is offered in the characters of Cherea and Scipio, who confront Caligula about his changed behavior.

And although Camus insisted that *The Misunderstanding* was not a pessimistic play—and that if Jan had identified himself, the tragedy would have been prevented—few critics view it that way, wherein there seems, with the assassination of Caligula at that play's conclusion, that the chance for some happiness in life exists among these minor characters.

THE REVOLT CYCLE

> The world I live in is loathsome to me, but I feel one with the men who suffer in it.
> —"Why Spain?" published in *Combat*, 1948.

In the early 1940s, Camus began writing for the French Resistance in a newspaper called *Combat*. During this time—after France's international embarrassment, and living under Nazi occupation and the collaborationist Vichy regime—Camus's thinking and philosophy inevitably became less nihilistic and solipsistic in nature. The war forced him to consider how one acts within the human community, what affect those acts have on the lives and condition of others, and upon what criteria to base such actions. In response, he began to write articles arguing against totalitarianism in any form, including his famous "Letters to A German Friend," a fictional correspondence wherein Camus explained why he could not blindly support a regime, without full knowledge, and approval, of the reasons for doing so. In the letters, readers detect Camus's movement beyond the absurd: "I continue to believe that this world has no ultimate meaning. But I know that something in it has meaning and that is man, because he is the only creature to insist on having one. This world has at least the truth of man, and our task is to provide its justification against fate itself ... With your scornful smile you will ask me: what do you mean by saving man? And with all my being I shout to you that I mean not mutilating him and yet giving a chance to the justice that man alone can conceive." We see here, then, that the writer previously concerned with his own fate was thus replaced by one concerned with justice, measured action, and his place among men.

Of course, just as the "absurd" required a tailored definition, so too does Camus's version of "revolt." As David Zane Mairowitz reminds us, we normally revolt with "unrestrained freedom, with violence or aggression, at the very least a clash between rebellious forces and the status quo. Revolt goes beyond any law or morality or reason or religion which attempts to hold it down. Yet ... Camus reins in the word to align it with moderation" (Mairowitz, 131). Indeed, Camus wanted justice, but only if it didn't go beyond the bounds of decency and human dignity.

In 1941, though, when Camus began writing his novel, *The Plague*, his notion of revolt was only in its nascent stages. Finally published in 1947, and set in Oran—a French city in Algeria with its back to the sea—the novel follows a local doctor, Rieux, from his initial discovery of dead rats all around the city, to the full-blown onset of the plague, which causes the city to be closed off from the rest of the world for over a year. Other characters in the novel include a Jesuit priest, Father Panaloux; a justice-seeking drifter named Tarrou; a clerk named Grand who struggles daily to rewrite the first sentence of his novel; a crook, Cottard, who is relieved by, and encourages, the town's confinement because it protects him; and a journalist, Rambert, who had come to Oran to write an article, but who is desperate to escape the quarantine.

Critics have noted the strange, extremely self-conscious mysteriousness of Camus's narrator, revealing a character (and, not insignificantly, a creator) who is cautious and unsure about his place and function among people. Long passages throughout the narrative reveal an anxiety-riddled storyteller, straining to do the right thing by the story and the people involved: "Next day, Tarrou set to work and enrolled a first team of workers, soon to be followed by many others. However, it is not the narrator's intention to ascribe to these sanitary groups more importance than their due. Doubtless today many of our fellow citizens are apt to yield to the temptation of exaggerating the services they rendered. But the narrator is inclined to think that by attributing over-importance to praiseworthy actions one may, by implication, be paying indirect but potent homage to the worse side of human nature." This sort of strident self-justification and reach for objectivity continues, in this instance, for a page, thus demonstrating repeatedly that Rieux, like Camus, struggles with both being a part, and remaining outside, of the community in which he lives and works.

Other critics examine how the novel works as an allegory. Most agree that the plague represents the Nazis in France during the occupation, but the (in)effectiveness of this framework fuels more critical discussion. Steven G. Kellman, for instance, notes that Nazis were human beings committing evil, while the plague was a force of nature. He states, "Metaphysical questions are not always interchangeable with social ones. Our ethical responsibilities in responding to despotism or disease are different" (Kellman, 94). E. Freeman agrees, using a specific character to make the point:

> The petty profiteer Cottard has his reasons for welcoming the plague but he does not on his own symbolize the not inconsiderable proportion of the French population who supported Vichy and the collaboration for both practical and ideological reasons. He is a marginal figure, in no way constituting a threat to the resistance offered by Rieux, Tarrou, and others. Not all of the men and women who collaborated with the Nazis were crooks and opportunists: some, no doubt misguided in their political calculations, believed with great sincerity that they were saving French lives while waiting for a better chance to strike back. This whole element of political ambiguity is lacking in [*The Plague*] (Freeman, 83).

Also, because Camus suffered from bouts of tuberculosis on and off during this time, other critics instead chose to view the novel as a kind of examination of how disease attacks the physical body, thus highlighting the conflict between the physical and the intellectual being.[6] And just as was true with *The Stranger*, the issue of justice and judgment looms over *The Plague*. In one moment, after the magistrate's young son succumbs to the plague, Tarrou feels sympathy and yet asks, in his diary, "Who can help a judge?" Thus, again, in this Godless world, the pretense of being a judge is rendered meaningless; in such a context, human judges can have no power over nature.

The year after *The Plague* arrived on shelves, Camus wrote and (unsuccessfully) produced a play called *State of Siege*, a modern day morality play about totalitarianism. A character called the Plague, in human form, comes with his secretary to a town in Spain, where he enlists the help of a misanthropic, drunken dwarf named Nada to take over and organize the town, frightening the people into submission through random, unprovoked deaths.[7] Camus, as Philip Thody notes, is opposed to dictatorships of any kind, right- or left-leaning, and set the play in Spain to condemn the actions of the Church there. Readers should also note that again, in this play, the nearby water is depicted as a symbol of freedom, as well as eroticized, similar to Camus's early lyrical essays. In the first act, the chorus says, "The sea is calling us to happy places without walls or gates, to shores whose virgin sands are cool as maidens' lips, and where our eyes grow dazzled gazing seaward ... To the untrammeled waves, to clean, bright water, the shining winds of freedom!"

And although the play is typically dark, there are moments of humor, which, Camus admitted in one interview, was the element that readers and theatergoers most often missed in his work. Humor appears in "State of Siege" when Camus condemns the ticky-tacky details of bureaucracy, as he does during this exchange between the Plague's secretary and the Fisherman:

THE FISHERMAN [with rising exasperation]: I've been up to the office on the first floor and they told me to come back here. It seems I have to get a certificate of existence before I can get a certificate of health.
THE SECRETARY: That goes without saying.
THE FISHERMAN: "Goes without saying!" What do you mean by that?
THE SECRETARY: Why, it proves that this city is beginning to reap the benefits of a strong administration. We

start with the premises that you are guilty. But that's not enough; you must learn to feel, yourselves, that you are guilty. And you won't feel guilty until you are tired. So we weary you out, that's all. Once you are really tired, tired to death in fact, everything will run quite smoothly.

THE FISHERMAN: Anyhow, is there some way of getting this damned certificate of existence?

THE SECRETARY: Well, it really looks as if you couldn't. You see, you need to get a certificate of health first, before you are given a certificate of existence. It's a sort of deadlock, isn't it?

THE FISHERMAN: Then—what?

THE SECRETARY: Then you have to fall back on our good will. But like most sorts of good will ours is of limited duration. Thus we may grant you this certificate as a special favor. Only I warn you it will be valid for one week only. After that, we'll see ...

This sort of "who's on first"-style of biting repartee is an anomaly in Camus's writing,[8] but clearly, his intention here was to inject some humor into otherwise bleak proceedings.

The play's hero, Diego, ends up thwarting the Plague by confronting him without fear, but he is too late. Victoria, his fiancée, has already been killed, and Diego makes a deal with the Plague: his life for Victoria's. Camus's longtime mistress, Maria Cesarès, played Victoria, but to no avail; the play was an instant flop, and critics have since viewed it as yet another of Camus's unproducable plays, condemning it as self-righteously didactic, melodramatic, and downright dull. It does, nonetheless, fit into Camus's revolt cycle, and introduces an idea of great importance within the other works within the cycle: that of a willingness to offer your own life in exchange for taking another—a small step away from Tarrou, who rejected all killing for any reason in *The Plague*—so that a sense of justice and balance is maintained, as well as the idea of necessary limits to power.

The next play, *The Just Assassins*, produced the following year, builds on this notion. Based loosely on a true story, the play's setting is 1905 Russia, where a small group of revolutionaries have plotted to assassinate the Grand Duke Sergei Alexandrovitch, uncle of Tsar

Nicholas II. Yanek Kaliayev, called the Poet, is the man assigned to throw the bomb, and he is willing to give his life for the cause, knowing that he will be arrested and executed after the assassination. However, at the beginning, he comes to Dora (his lover), Boris, Voinov, and Stepan, and explains that he could not bring himself to throw the bomb because the Grand Duke's young niece and nephew rode in the carriage with him. This brings Kaliayev into conflict with Stepan, an absolutist regarding the revolution. Memorably, Stepan says to Dora, "Not until the day comes when we stop sentimentalizing about children will the revolution triumph, and we be masters of the world." And even though the group eventually decides that Kaliayev did the right thing by withholding the bomb, Stepan stridently disagrees, stating his willingness to kill multitudes now for the sake of a potentially better future, thus disregarding all those people currently living—a pet point of condemnation for Camus that will spearhead his objections to communism. One scene demonstrates these ideological distinctions in action:

> STEPAN: ... Just because Yanek couldn't bring himself to kill these two, thousands of Russian children will go on dying of starvation for years to come. Have you ever seen children dying of starvation? I have. And to be killed by a bomb is a pleasant death compared with that. But Yanek never saw children starving to death. He saw only the Grand Duke's pair of darling little lapdogs. Aren't you sentient human beings? Or are you living like animals for the moment only? In that case by all means indulge in charity and cure each petty suffering that meets your eye; but don't meddle with revolution, for its task is to cure all sufferings present and to come.
> DORA: Yanek's ready to kill the Grand Duke because his death may help to bring nearer the time when Russian children will no longer die of hunger. That in itself is none too easy for him. But the death of the Grand Duke's niece and nephew won't prevent any child from dying of hunger. Even in destruction there's a right way and a wrong way— and there are limits.
> STEPAN [vehemently]: There are no limits! The truth is

that you don't believe in the revolution, any of you. [All, except Kaliayev, rise to their feet.] No, you don't believe in it. If you did believe in it sincerely, with all your hearts; if you felt sure that, by dint of our struggles and sacrifices, some day we shall build up a new Russia, redeemed from despotism, a land of freedom that will gradually spread out over the earth; and if you felt convinced that then and only then, freed from his masters and his superstitions, man will at last look up toward the sky, a god in his own right—how, I ask you, could the deaths of two children be weighed in the balance against such a faith?

Interestingly, the situation thematically recalls a moment in *The Plague*, wherein Dr. Rieux watches the magistrate's young son fight against the disease only to succumb to it in the end; this causes Rieux to confront the Jesuit priest (Panaloux), asking why, if there is a God, He would let children suffer this way. Thus, in two separate works by Camus, endangered children cause a crisis of faith (in God in one case, in communism in the other), and thus, Camus's rhetoric about limits is communicated in similar ways in the Revolt cycle.

The Just Assassins, however, though a commercial success, was not a critical success, especially because many who were sympathetic to communism—largely intellectuals—felt defensive about the content. But all this was only a prelude to the bomb Camus himself was about to throw at them: *The Rebel*.

The product of years of work, *The Rebel*, published in 1951, is a long, somewhat unwieldy philosophical tract.[9] Camus's primary goal with this work, as summed up by critic Philip Thody, is to elucidate two paradoxes: "that the greatest rebel is tempted by the greatest conformity" and "that revolt, which at first sight appears to be the rejection of all limits, is in fact a demand for a limit" (*Albert Camus*, 60). To respond to these ideas, Camus champions revolt on the individual level, rather than as a mass or large group—thus alluding to and critiquing the herd-like movement of intellectuals toward communism; and regarding the second paradox—as witnessed in *The Just Assassins*— he advocates maintaining common sense decency and morality while aspiring to eliminate injustice. (In *The Rebel*, he referred to the real-life occurrence depicted in *The Just Assassins* as when "the spirit of revolt meets compassion for the last time in our history.") Obviously, according to Camus, the problem with Stepan in *The Just Assassins* is that he is so rigidly focused on an idealized future that he is willing to commit, and thus reduce himself to, acts of barbarity against those living in the present in order to achieve it.

In *The Rebel*, Camus craftily confronted his peers by meeting them on their own terms and contending with the ideas of those they admired—including Nietzsche, Marquis de Sade, Rimbaud, Lautreamont, Marx, and Hegel. Camus reserves most of his attention, however, for Hegel, in order to respond to his idea that any and all actions may be justified by the scope of history; that is, if the greater good will ultimately be viewed as having been served by present evils, than any acts of cruelty or murder may be justified. In this way, Hegel glorified the State above all else, and when Marxists used Hegel's ideas, Camus believed that the movement became its own religion, with history as its god. In Camus's eyes, no totalitarian regime was good, even if, as was true for the ideal of communism, the goal was justice for the everyman.

Responses to *The Rebel* were mixed—though it sold well—but what the work is most famous for is precipitating Camus's (very public) break from Sartre. They had never been wholly aligned in their thinking,[10] but with the publication of *The Rebel* came a scathing review, written by Francis Jeanson, in Sartre's magazine, *Les Temps Moderne*. Camus wrote a heated letter in response, addressing it to Sartre, that ran sixteen pages in length. The magazine ran the letter, along with Sartre's nineteen page response (and an even longer response from Jeanson, the reviewer). The broad-scaled intellectual backlash overwhelmed Camus, who came to be viewed by many as a bourgeois sell-out. Although Camus's humanist ideas might have found greater purchase during the movements of the '60s, he appeared to be wholly out of step with the predominant thinking of his own time. Naturally, isolation from his literary and intellectual peers only added to Camus's sense of solitude, but even more social exile was to come, as the issue of colonialism in Algeria reached a violent crisis.

A Dry Spell

Everyone wants the man who is still searching to have already reached his conclusions. A thousand voices are already telling him what he has found, and yet he knows that he hasn't found anything. Should he search on and let them talk? Of course. But, from time to time, one must defend himself.

—"The Enigma," 1950

In 1952, Camus began to write what would be his last works: a novel called *The First Man*; short stories that would make up the collection *Exile and the Kingdom*; and a play combining the stories of Don Juan and Faust, which he talked about for years but never completed. These works were to compose what Camus planned as a love cycle, a theme hinted at in his essay, "Return to Tipasa," released in 1954 in a collection of essays, called *Summer*: "there is only misfortune in not being loved; there is misery in not loving." *Summer*, in fact, was the only publication for Camus, aside from newspaper articles, between the years 1951 and 1957, though he was writing off and on throughout this period of time.

One reason for his publishing inactivity was his involvement, and personal heartbreak, regarding the Algerian question. Sparked by the 1954 battle of Dien Bien Phu—wherein Vietnamese rebels overthrew French rule to resume control of Indochina—nationalists in Algeria (the Front de liberation nationale, or FLN) began to organize. Soon, 400,000 French soldiers were in Algeria, and terrorist violence broke out in Camus's homeland, where his mother still lived, despite Camus's repeated pleadings for her to move to Paris. Camus, trying to be the voice of moderation and reason, argued that the French should remain in Algeria, but that Arabs should also have more rights and participation in government. He insisted that the two groups could live in harmony. Though he sympathized with the Arabs, he still believed them to be better off in the hands of France, and because the first French had emigrated there in the mid-1800s, Camus felt that those families who had raised generations there, like his own, should be considered "indigenous." (Camus wrote thirty-five articles on the Algerian crisis in 1955, for *l'Express*, a daily newspaper, which works in part to explain his lack of literary publications.) Unfortunately, though—much like the outcome of a tie in sports—Camus's middle-of-the-road ideas satisfied no one, and both nationalists and colonialists spoke out against him.

Finally, in 1956, while Camus was in Algiers to speak in support of his own proposal—a "Civil Truce," which asked both groups to sign a document stating that they would not attack the innocent civilian population—he received death threats, and a rock was thrown through a window. Shortly after this tense event, Camus decided to silence himself on the topic, which, of course, caused him to be vilified anew in the press, which then painted Camus as a traitor to both France and Algeria, as well as a coward.

Meanwhile, Camus's wife, Francine Faure, tried twice to kill herself. Though she was never happy about Camus's philandering, she accepted it for years without complaint. During this time, though, she suffered from serious clinical depression. She was hospitalized, and Camus's feelings of guilt regarding this woman he loved—albeit fraternally—consumed him. Many critics argue that it was indeed this guilt that led him to write *The Fall*. Originally intended as a novella for inclusion in the story collection *Exile and the Kingdom*, the piece expanded into a novel in its own right, published in 1956. Though little known among today's readers, many critics consider this novel to be Camus's finest and most complex work, and some claim that the feverish way in which Camus wrote it left it standing alone, outside of his planned literary cycle.[11]

The Fall's narrator, Jean-Baptiste Clamence, tells the story as one long monologue to an unidentified man he befriends in an Amsterdam bar. Formerly a lawyer, Clamence tells of how smoothly he conducted himself in his life years before; how he used women for his pleasures, lied to them, and made them promise to love no one else while quickly he found another mistress; how he fought for clients whom he could present as victims of judges in the courtroom, thus making himself feel noble for defending the underdog; how he charmed and oozed his way through society, never investing or giving himself to anything. But all this changes when Clamence sees a woman about to jump off a bridge and fails to stop her. Suddenly, Clamence feels the weight of his actions (or inaction, as the case may be), and this guilt drives him to leave his life, since he could no longer lead it in the same manner. As critic René Girard noted, Clamence's "real desire was not to save his clients but to prove his moral superiority by discrediting the judges" (Girard, 80). For this reason, many critics have viewed *The Fall* as a work in which Camus critiques himself, both in terms of his work—profiting from telling others how they should and shouldn't act, and judging others for, well, judging others—as well as his behavior during the course of his marriage, and his feelings of culpability regarding Francine's suicide attempts.

Though he repeatedly denied that *The Fall* was in any way biographical, Olivier Todd reports that "Camus's denials were meant to protect his family and his private life," adding that Francine "and several other readers knew that the episode in [*The Fall*] when a young woman throws herself into the Seine from the Pont des Arts referred to Francine's suicide attempts in Oran and Paris in 1954" (Todd, 345, 342). Indeed, one of Francine's attempts involved her "fall" from a window, thus making the book's much-discussed title that much more poignant, most likely, to those few in Camus's inner circle.

Of course, critics have also made much of the novel's religious/biblical overtones, beginning with the narrator's name— Camus even has the narrator refer to his story as a "cry in the wilderness," just like John the Baptist—as well as the title, which automatically assumes symbolic weight. Clamence's fall is from blissful ignorance to self-awareness, self-loathing, and knowledge, thus mirroring the original fall in the Garden of Eden. In addition, many think that near the end of Camus's abruptly-ended life, he was considering adopting religion—Catholicism specifically—and use textual clues in *The Fall* to make their case; naturally, though, just as many critics argue that Camus wove numerous religious elements into the text with the aim of achieving irony, thereby undercutting its relevance.

Most importantly, however, the issue of judgment arises again, and it is of central importance. Camus appears to have evolved from contempt for all who claim to be judges to a more self-aware conclusion: "since we are all judges, we are all guilty before one another, all Christs in our mean manner, one by one crucified, always without knowing."

THE INCOMPLETE LOVE CYCLE

In March of 1957, Camus's short story collection, *Exile and the Kingdom*, was released. Four of the six stories take place in Algeria, and they reveal a writer becoming more concerned with narrative craft, experimenting with different methods of narration, structures, and topics. Many critics consider the collection invaluable in that Camus (perhaps finally) emphasized storytelling over philosophy and politics, thus infusing the stories with a human warmth that had been missing in previous works.

The first story, "An Adulterous Woman," is told from the perspective of a woman—the first and only female narrator to appear in Camus's career—who travels Algeria with her salesman husband, but feels a nagging restlessness in her comfortable but loveless marriage, so she sneaks out in the middle of the night to look at the stars and the desert; her adultery is with the landscape, the place itself, but she eventually returns to her bed, resigned. The second story, "The Renegade," is told from the point of view of a recently-converted missionary who goes into a dangerous part of Africa and endures torture, including getting his tongue cut out; he then embraces evil just as he had wholly, suddenly embraced God, and at the conclusion, he lies in wait to kill the missionary sent out to take his place. (Camus claimed, in a letter to a friend, that this story was about intellectuals, whose allegiances and absolutism shifted too easily, and who sniped at each other.) In "The Silent Men," an Algerian Frenchman who works as a cooper returns to his job after a failed strike. (At the cooperage, critics note, there are Spaniards, Arabs, and Frenchmen, a mixed, poor, honest community that makes up Camus's ideal of Algeria as he wished it to be.) The workers treat the boss coldly, which angers him, but then, the boss's young daughter falls seriously ill, causing the men to remain silent. The difference, of course, is that their silence changes from one of cold refusal to one of speechless sympathy. Critics here note not only the championing of the dignity of the working class, but also the beginning of Camus's descent into the more blatantly personal, since much of the description of the cooperage resembles that of his Uncle Etienne, whom he helped at work twice a week as a child.

The fourth story, "The Guest," may perhaps be the most famous, and many critics considered it the strongest story in the collection. In it, a French Algerian schoolteacher, living alone in the schoolhouse, is left with an Arab arrested for murder. The teacher is ordered to deliver the Arab to the police station in a nearby town the next morning. Daru, the teacher, tells the officer that he will not do it, though he knows this will get him in trouble. Nonetheless, he lets the Arab stay overnight, secretly hoping that the Arab would escape, but he doesn't even try. The next morning, the teacher walks with the Arab, gives him money, and tells him that one path leads to Nomads, who would take him in, and the other way leads to the police. Daru leaves him, and after a few minutes, he watches the Arab walk toward the town and the police station. And upon Daru's return, a message written on the blackboard says, "You handed over our brother. You will pay for this." Critics discuss the complexity of the Algerian crisis being examined here, as well as the position in which Camus found himself when speaking out on the topic. Just as Daru is condemned by not agreeing to take the Arab to the police, he is also condemned by giving the Arab a say in his own fate; regardless of his good intentions or understandable actions, he is guilty on both sides. (Some even surmise that the Arab makes the choice he does so as to save his host, ironically, from being punished, only for this generous gesture to utterly backfire.) Still other critics note how this story includes the first (and only) individualized, more fleshed-out Arabic character that Camus ever created, thus demonstrating a new awareness of this lack in his work, and the inherent, if unintentional, racism it may suggest.

The fifth story, "The Artist at Work" tells the story of a painter in France who is wholly content creating art, regardless of whether he's successful or not. But he marries and becomes successful, and friends and hangers-on gather all day every day, and though he's still content, his work begins to suffer. He starts to move away from the people and the crowds, as his star descends in the art world, until he finally builds a loft, wherein he literally works above everyone in the apartment. But he grows depressed, can't produce anything, and at the end, his friend notes that the only thing on the canvas is a word in small letters, though he can't quite make it out: either "solidary" or "solitary." This push and pull that artists feel is something that shows up again and again in Camus's work and his notebooks. One has to be out in the world to stay in touch with it, and in order to create art from it, but at the same time, living in the isolation that's necessary to produce artistic work is nearly impossible, especially when the artist experiences success (as Camus did at a young age).

Finally, "The Growing Stone," a story critics view as one of the most optimistic pieces Camus ever wrote, tells the story of D'Arrast, an engineer coming to Africa to build a dam. After arriving—and receiving cold reception from all but the officials of the town—he's invited to attend a local holiday celebration, wherein a cook he meets has vowed to carry a one hundred pound stone on his back during the procession. The cook comes up short, and D'Arrast picks up the rock and takes it to the cook's family's tent, where he is invited to share in the meal. Again, critics have noted how this idealizes how, with compassion, different races of people can co-exist, revealing Camus's anxiety about the topic, as well as his hopes, in spite of his knowledge of the capacity for evil within human nature.

This denial also carried over into Camus's continued criticism of capital punishment. During the same year that *Exile and the Kingdom* was published, Camus wrote his famous essay, "Reflections on the Guillotine," which was included in a collection of similar essays compiled by novelist Arthur Koestler. Camus's arguments included: blaming the society that produced the criminals, human fallibility in making judgments, the hypocrisy behind the idea of capital punishment deterring criminals while the executions are committed in private, the role of alcohol (the makers of which go unpunished) in crimes, and the loss of basic human dignity suffered by the criminal. Camus's obsession regarding capital punishment appears to stem from a story his mother told him about his father (who died in World War I when Camus was only one year old), and he tells the story near the beginning of the essay. Apparently, a farmhand brutally killed a local farmer and his family, and Camus's father, Lucien, decided that he would attend this execution in support of the verdict. But Lucien returned, saying nothing and looking pale, and when he lay down on his bed, he started to vomit. This story convinced Camus that no matter what the crime, when one is faced with a living human being, one cannot stomach watching an execution. As Camus says in his essay, "When the extreme penalty simply causes vomiting on the part of the respectable citizen it is supposed to protect, how can anyone maintain that it is likely, as it ought to be, to bring more peace and order into the community?"

Regarding the topic of his father, Camus returned to it in the novel he was then working on, called *The First Man*, but in October 1957, everything got temporarily put on hold when Camus received the news that he had won the Nobel Prize. Not surprisingly, many still-bitter intellectuals attacked and criticized Camus in the Paris press, and some grumbled that he got it by default, for politically correct reasons (i.e., Camus's humanism was less threatening than, say, André Maulraux's

politics). Camus even considered refusing the award, but in the end—
with firm nudging from his publisher—he decided to accept.

Afterward, he adapted and produced an ambitious production of
Dostoyevsky's *The Possessed* in 1958, and he also resumed work on *The
First Man*, which he planned to expand into two volumes. His efforts
were cut short in January 1960, however, when Camus died in a car crash
at age forty-six. In the car was the working manuscript of the novel-in-
progress, but Camus's estate refused to publish the work until 1994,
thirty-four years after his death. In this uncorrected draft—which many
feel Camus would have subsequently doctored in order to make the story
less nakedly, plainly autobiographical—readers finally get a vivid glimpse
of Camus's personal experiences, specifically his childhood in Algeria.
He tells of his strict, vain, manipulative grandmother; his silent, distant,
hard-working mother; his schooling, which was his escape from an
unhappy home; and the family's extreme poverty, including, most
memorably, an anecdote about his grandmother. Camus had once taken
some money given to him for errands in order to attend a soccer match;
the lie he told his grandmother was that he'd dropped the money from
his pockets into the hole of the Turkish toilet. In horror, he then
watched his grandmother roll up her sleeve, preparing to try and retrieve
the money.

In addition to poverty, though, readers get vivid insights into the
central heartbreak of Camus's life: the inaccessibility of his mother.
Though Camus seems pained while recounting the visit to his father's
grave—where the realization that Camus was then older than his
twenty-nine-year-old father had been when he died strikes him
powerfully, and he decides to seek out his father and find out all he can
about him—nothing seems to approach the poignancy of the passages
about his mother. In one scene between Jacques, the main character, and
his mother, Camus wrote: "He was going to say: 'You're very beautiful,'
and he stopped himself. He had always thought that of his mother and
had never dared to tell her so. It was not that he feared being rebuffed
nor that he doubted such a compliment would please her. But it would
have meant breaching the invisible barrier behind which for all his life
he had seen her take shelter ..." Such moments leave the reader with the
impression that just as we were on the cusp of learning more about this
enigmatic, ever-evolving writer, his life abruptly ended.

CONCLUSION

> ... the world is nothing and the world is everything—this is the
> contradictory and tireless cry of every true artist, the cry that keeps
> him on his feet with eyes ever open and that, every once in a while,
> awakens for all in this world asleep the fleeting and insistent image
> of a reality we recognize without ever having known it.
>
> —"Create Dangerously," 1957

Camus's existence, from the outset of his life, lay among the fringe. He did not exactly belong among the indigenous, poor Arabs who populated North Africa, but neither was his family of the class of moneyed French colonialists who emigrated there and sought to "civilize" the Arabs. Instead, like the Mediterranean Sea itself, he lay somewhere between Algeria and France, always maintaining simultaneously his status as both an insider and an outsider—a position that permanently affected his literary style and colored his perspective.

And although Camus became far less detached in his writing style near the end of his short life, critics like S. Beynon John noted that his fixation on Greek myths and tragedies manifested itself in this "removed" style. Even works that are set in, or near, the present time have the feeling of an allegory or Greek tragedy, wherein people aren't psychologically realized, three dimensional beings with their own past, but are instead vehicles for beliefs or ideological systems. As John states, "Myth is a substitute for faith and the metaphors of religion, and myth, by its very nature, is anonymous and collective: it swallows up the individual life" ("Albert Camus" 91). Similarly, Paul de Man wrote that through the consistent depersonalization of Camus's style, the writer "always chose to hide behind the mask of a deliberate, controlled style or behind a pseudo-confessional tone that serves to obscure, rather than reveal, his true self" (de Man, 19).

However, as we review the progression of Camus's work and ideas, one can't help but feel that Camus, though possibly flawed as a thinker, was never less than honest with his readers, and that he hoped—by working through, on paper, his own questions—to find not only answers for himself, but to share them with his vexed, cynical, post-war fellow citizens. Camus viewed this as his job, a task he took very seriously; for we see a rigid intolerance in Camus's notebooks for personal experience or anecdotes, allowing only things relevant to work to appear. This reveals, as de Man notes, "the solitude that torments Camus is most of all an estrangement from what he considers his authentic former self" (de Man, 22).

Thus, although Camus began with questions regarding nature and man's limits in the physical world, and moved on to questioning his function in the larger human community in times of crisis, he ended by arriving at his own memories, still perhaps searching for connection to others by way of finally, hopefully, understanding himself. And despite criticisms incessantly voiced during Camus's life (and since), we should note that great minds are very often out of sync with their times. Camus's reservations regarding communism were obviously well-grounded, we now see in retrospect, and his stance on Algeria, while perhaps idealistic, was both honest and understandable, and his "Civilian Truce" was wholly meritorious in principle. Such hindsight should thus render Camus's intellectual bravery imminently laudable. He likely knew the consequences of publishing *The Rebel*, but he did so anyway, cutting himself off from Sartre's pack, despite subsequent personal attacks from that powerful intellectual lobby. This is not to say, of course, that Camus's intellect exceeded his peers, but unlike others, he willingly admitted when his ideas changed and why, and he always stood by the controversial conclusions he so publicly struggled to attain. As critic Susan Tarrow put it, Camus's works will remain perpetually relevant "not because he had the 'right' answers, but because he persistently asked the right questions" (Tarrow, 200).

NOTES

1. French immigrants in Algeria were called "pied-noirs" because of the black shoes many of them wore, which the native Algerians had never seen.

2. Camus resisted the label "existentialist" all his life, claiming that from the very first—including *The Myth of Sisyphus*—he was *responding* to the existentialists, not aligning himself with them. (His protests grew particularly adamant later in his life, though this may have been caused by the existentialists's strong communist leanings, which Camus intensely disdained.) However, because the definition of existentialism is somewhat broad, it appears to most scholars that Camus embraced the basic precepts of that school of thought (atheism, nihilism, life's

meaninglessness) enough so that despite his protests, he still most often gets categorized with them. And although his regard for nature and his early Hellenist tendencies do set him apart, as well as his emphasis in later work on a specific morality, his name is still almost always paired with Sartre.

3. In fact, the only external event in Camus's life that appears to have merited mention in his notebooks—as mentioned in Thody's footnotes—was a job offer to teach, which Camus turned down,

4. According to biographer Olivier Todd, Camus found the "positive side" of his sickness by thinking of it as "a remedy against death, because it prepares us for death, creating an apprenticeship whose first step is self-pity. Illness supports man in the great attempt to shirk the fact that he will surely die." (And, really, who wouldn't be cheered by this?)

5. Critics differ as to whether Zagreus conspires with Meursault in his own murder.

6. This became even more relevant in the 1980s and 90s, while America was in the throes of an AIDS epidemic; Camus's novel received renewed attention at this time.

7. Many critics see Nada as representative of left-wing intellectuals of the time—those who, in the eyes of Camus, justify totalitarianism in the absence of established values.

8. Camus also includes a moment of humor in *Caligula*, wherein the emperor demands his poets to compose a piece on the theme of death on the spot, and then he cuts down the overblown, melodramatic attempts as though he were hosting a kind of game show.

9. One reason for the lack of fluidity in *The Rebel* is that some sections were previously published as articles, so when they were pasted together with others, the book assumed a stilted feel.

10. Sartre had his own doubts about communism, but he, along with other intellectuals, saw no better alternative for achieving justice for the most people, specifically the disenfranchised.

11. Early notes do, however, hint that Camus at one point had in mind a Nemesis cycle—Nemesis, in Greek mythology, being the goddess of divine retribution—within which *The Fall* would certainly fit.

Works Cited

Bree, Germaine, ed. Introduction. *Camus: A Collection of Critical Essays.* Englewood Cliffs, NJ: Prentice-Hall, Inc., 1962.1–10.

Barthes, Roland. *Writing Degree Zero.* tr. Annette Lavers and Colin Smith. New York: Hill & Wang, 1968.

Camus, Albert. *Caligula & Three Other Plays.* tr. Stuart Gilbert. New York: Alfred A. Knopf, Inc., 1958.

———. *Collected Plays.* tr. Stuart Gilbert. London: Hamish Hamilton Ltd., 1965.

———. *Exile and the Kingdom.* tr. Justin O'Brien. New York: Alfred A. Knopf, Inc., 1958.

———. *The Fall.* tr. Justin O'Brien. New York: Alfred A. Knopf, Inc., 1957.

———. *The First Man.* tr. David Hapgood. New York: Alfred A. Knopf, Inc., 1995.

———. *A Happy Death.* tr. Richard Howard. New York: Alfred A. Knopf, Inc., 1972.

———. *Lyrical and Critical Essays.* tr. Ellen Conroy Kennedy. New York: Alfred A. Knopf, Inc., 1968.

———. *The Myth of Sisyphus and Other Essays.* tr. Justin O'Brien. New York: Alfred A. Knopf, Inc., 1969.

———. *Notebooks 1935–1951.* tr. Philip Thody. New York: Marlowe & Company, 1963.

———. *The Plague.* tr. Stuart Gilbert. New York: Vintage International, 1975.

———. *The Rebel: An Essay on Man in Revolt.* tr. Anthony Bower. New York: Vintage Books, 1956.

———. *Resistance, Rebellion, & Death.* tr. Justin O'Brien. New York: Alfred A. Knopf, Inc., 1961.

———. *The Stranger.* tr. Stuart Gilbert. New York: Alfred A. Knopf, Inc., 1974.

Erickson, John. "Albert Camus and North Africa: A Discourse of Exteriority." *Critical Essays on Albert Camus.* Ed. Bettina L. Knapp. Boston: G. K. Hall & Co., 1988. 73–87.

Freeman, E. *The Theatre of Albert Camus: A Critical Study.* London: Methuen & Co. Ltd., 1971.

Girard, René. "Camus's Stranger Retried." *Albert Camus.* ed. Harold Bloom. Modern Critical Views Series. New York: Chelsea House Publishers, 1988. 79–106.

John, S. Beynon."Albert Camus: A British View." *Camus: A Collection of Critical Essays*. Englewood Cliffs, NJ: Prentice-Hall, Inc., 1962. 1–10.

——. "Image and Symbol in the Work of Albert Camus." *Camus: A Collection of Critical Essays*. Englewood Cliffs, NJ: Prentice-Hall, Inc., 1962. 1–10.

Kellman, Steven G. *The Plague: Fiction and Resistance*. Twayne's Masterwork Series. New York: Twayne Publishers, 1993.

Lottman, Herbert R. *Albert Camus: A Biography*. New York: Doubleday & Co., 1979.

Mairowitz, David Zane and Alain Korkos. *Introducing Camus*. Cambridge: Icon Books Ltd., 1996.

Man, Paul de. "The Mask of Albert Camus: *Notebooks 1942–1951*." *Albert Camus*. ed. Harold Bloom. Modern Critical Views Series. New York: Chelsea House Publishers, 1988. 19–26.

Quilliot, Roger. "Albert Camus's Algeria." *Camus: A Collection of Critical Essays*. Englewood Cliffs, NJ: Prentice-Hall, Inc., 1962. 38–47.

Tarrow, Susan. *Exile from the Kingdom: A Political Rereading of Albert Camus*. University: University of Alabama Press, 1985.

Thody, Philip. *Albert Camus: A Study of His Work*. London: Hamish Hamilton Ltd., 1957.

——. Introduction. *Notebooks 1935–1951*. tr. Philip Thody. New York: Marlowe & Company, 1963. *v–xi*.

Todd, Olivier. *Albert Camus: A Life*. tr. Benjamin Ivry. New York: Alfred A. Knopf, Inc., 1997.

PAUL DE MAN

The Mask of Albert Camus:
Notebooks 1942–1951

The subtle but radical change that separates the intellectual atmosphere of the fifties from that of the sixties could well be measured by one's attitude towards the work and the person of Albert Camus. During his lifetime he was for many an exemplary figure; his work bears many traces of the doubts and agonies that such an exalted position inevitably carries with it. He has not ceased to be so: In several recent literary essays, written by men whose formative years coincided with the period of Camus's strongest influence, the impact of his presence can still be strongly felt. On the other hand, one can well imagine how he might prove disappointing to a new generation, not because this generation lacks the experience that shaped Camus's world, but because the interpretation he gave of his own experience lacks clarity and insight. That Sartre and Merleau-Ponty, different from each other as they are, seem more closely attuned to the modern temper is by itself no proof of their superiority. Nor indeed does this make Camus necessarily the defender of permanent values. Before we can blame our times for moving away from him, we must clarify our notion of what he represents.

The publication of the *Notebooks* is a useful addition to the understanding of a writer who, in his fiction, always chose to hide behind the mask of a deliberate, controlled style or behind a pseudo-

From *The New York Review of Books* 5, no. 10 (23 December 1965). © 1965 by NYREV, Inc. Reprinted by permission.

confessional tone that serves to obscure, rather than to reveal, his true self. The "I" that addresses the reader in *The Stranger* and in *The Fall*, and the collective "we" of *The Plague*, are never to be directly identified with the voice of Camus; in accordance with the tradition of the novel, the author reserves the right to keep his interpretations of characters and events implicit and ambivalent. The genre of the novel is, by definition, oblique, and no one thinks of blaming Cervantes for the fact that, up to this very day, critics cannot agree whether he was for or against Don Quixote. More contemporary figures, however, are not allowed the same immunity especially if, like Camus, they openly intervene in public and political matters and claim to experience personal conflicts that are typical of the historical situation in general. In such cases, one is certainly entitled to look for utterances in which the true commitment (or the true uncertainty) of the writer is revealed.

Camus's *Notebooks* do not offer an easy key to the understanding of an irresolute man. In this second volume of his private notes—the first volume of the *Notebooks*, covering the period from May 1935 to February 1942, has also been published in English—Camus's personal reserve has increased rather than diminished, and the lack of intimacy or of self-display is both admirable and unusual. There is nothing here of the abandon, the indiscretion of many intimate journals, very little self-justification or, for that matter, self-analysis. The second volume of the *Notebooks* deals with the period from January 1942 till March 1951, during which the main events in Camus's personal, public, and literary life took place: his forced stay in occupied France after the Allied landing in North Africa, his participation in the Resistance and subsequent political activity as editor of *Combat*, the considerable success of his novels and plays, which made him one of the most influential writers of the post-war era. It is during this period that he wrote *The Plague* and the ambitious essay *Man in Revolt* (*The Rebel* in its American edition), which interprets the modern predicament as a historical conflict of values. It was also during this period that Camus's inner conflicts and hesitations gained in intensity, leading to a growing retreat from public action, the eventual break with Sartre, and the combination of bitterness and lucidity that one finds in *The Fall*.

Obviously it was a very rich and complex period—but only the remotest echoes filter through to the pages of these notebooks. Readers who expect revelations, strong opinions, anecdotes, and the like will be disappointed. Even the most unsettling personal episodes in Camus's life appear in remote and indirect perspectives. For instance, when he suffered an unexpected recurrence of his early tuberculosis in 1949, his reaction to the event appears in the *Notebooks* only in the form of a poignant note quoted from one of Keats's last letters, written while he was dying in Rome of the same disease. The example, one among many, shows how remote the notebooks are from a personal journal. They are essentially workbooks, comparable to the sketch pads that certain painters carry with them, in which reactions to the outside world are recorded only insofar as they are relevant to the work in progress.

The *Notebooks* consist primarily of outlines for future plays or novels, notes on current reading, early versions of passages, records of situations or remarks observed at the time and stored away for later reference. Camus made considerable use of these notes: many key passages from later books first appear here, frequently as brief notations without further comment or reflections. For a student of Camus's work, the *Notebooks* thus contain much important information. The present collection will prove indispensable, especially to interpreting *The Plague* and *The Rebel*. Together with the notes and variants established by Roger Quilliot for the *Pléiade* edition of the novels and plays, the *Notebooks* give us the kind of information about the genesis of Camus's writing that is ordinarily made available only many decades after an author's death.

But the *Notebooks* can also serve a less specialized function, and help towards a general consideration of Camus's development. No matter how rigorous the reserve, how decorous the self-restraint, a fuller image nevertheless shines through these pages, though more by what they leave unsaid than by what they bring to light. One is struck, for instance, by the considerable difference in tone between the later pages of the *Notebooks* and those contained in the previous volume. The earlier remarks frequently had the spontaneous, lyrical quality of ideas and impressions revealed for their own sake. No deep gulf separates the actual person from the writer, and what is of interest to the one also serves the other. When, in 1940, Camus describes his reactions to the city of Oran he does so with a vivacity of perception that brings the city to life even more effectively than in the opening pages of *The Plague*. The pages on Oran in the 1940 notebook are felicitous in themselves and useful to his later work as well. As the notebooks progress, and especially after the war, such happy conjunctions between the writer's experience and his literary work become less and less frequent: Camus deliberately tore himself away from his natural inclinations and forced upon himself a number of alien concerns. As a result, the *Notebooks* reflect an increasing feeling of estrangement and solitude. One feels an almost obsessive commitment to work, a rejection of any moment of private experience as self-indulgence. The man and the writer have less and less in common, and the writer owed it to his avocation to keep repressing his personal life:

> Only by a continual effort can I create. My tendency is to drift toward immobility. My deepest, surest inclination lies in silence and the daily routine.... But I know that I stand erect through that very effort and that if I ceased to believe in it for a single moment I should roll over the precipice. This is how I avoid illness and renunciation, raising my head with all my strength to breathe and to conquer. This is my way of despairing and this is my way of curing myself.

The resolution undoubtedly has moral grandeur, but it requires the constant rejection of a personal quality which is, in fact, not just oriented towards silence and mechanical routine. Outcries of rebellion against solitude punctuate the notebooks and give them a more somber tone than is found in any of Camus's dramatic or fictional works. Optimistic assertions about the necessity of dialogue and the ultimate value of the individual are interspersed with notations of despair: "Unbearable solitude—I cannot believe it or resign myself to it"; "Utter solitude. In the urinal of a major railway station at 1 a.m." The spontaneous elation that inspires the pages on Algiers, Oran, and the cities of Italy in the early notebooks has been replaced by this note of despair and alienation: for the solitude that torments Camus is most of all an estrangement from what he considers his authentic former self. The more he gets involved with others, with social issues and public forms of thought and action, the more he feels a loss of contact with his true being.

This evolution is so frequent in modern literature that it certainly does not, by itself, warp Camus's interpretation of his times. His loneliness is genuine, not a pose; the scruples that haunted him while he was being increasingly rewarded by a society in which he participated so little are apparent in many passages of the *Notebooks*. It cannot be said of him, as of the hero of *The Fall*—who is an amalgamation of several contemporaries with certain personal traits of Camus himself—that he lived in bad faith, buying a good conscience by substituting for genuine abnegation the stance and the rhetoric of sacrifice. If one suspects that Camus was thriving on his exposure of contemporary nihilism, enjoying an intellectual position that claimed to suffer from the absurdity of the age while making this absurdity fashionable—then the note of real disarray sounded throughout the *Notebooks* should dispel such doubts. The paradox in which Camus was caught is both more interesting and more intricate: it is not his good faith but the quality of his insight that is to be questioned.

Camus very rightly made his own isolation the basis of his negative diagnosis of the present course of history. He then interpreted this isolation as a conflict between the individual and history. There never is any doubt in his mind that the source of all values resides in the individual, in his ability to resist the monstrous encroachments that history makes upon his integrity. And for Camus this integrity, which he strove to shelter from totalitarian and deterministic forms of thought, is founded in man's capacity for personal happiness. Camus's concern for others is always protective: he wants to keep intact a potential happiness, a possible fulfillment that every individual carries within him. Socialism is for him an organization of society that safeguards this potentiality: hence his enthusiasm for Belinski's "individualistic socialism" against Hegel's claims for totality and universality. The source of this conviction, however, is to be found in Camus's own experience, and the quality of his thought depends, finally, on the intrinsic quality of his inner experience.

On this point, early works such as *Noces* and especially the earlier *Notebooks* dating from before *The Stranger*, are highly instructive. Camus's sense of personal fulfillment is perhaps most clearly revealed in the exalted pages he wrote in September 1937 during a visit to the cities of Tuscany:

> We lead a difficult life. We don't always succeed in adjusting our actions to our vision of things.... We have to labor and to struggle to reconquer solitude. But then, one day, the earth shows its primitive and naive smile. Then it is as if struggles

and life itself were suddenly erased. Millions of eyes have
contemplated this landscape before, but for me it is like the
smile of the world. In the deepest sense of the term, it takes
me outside myself.... The world is beautiful, and nothing else
matters. The great truth the world patiently teaches us is that
heart and mind are nothing. And that the stone warmed by
the sun, or the cypress magnified by the blue of heaven are
the limits of the only world in which being right has
meaning: nature without man.... It is in that sense that I
understand the word "nakedness" [*dénuement*]. "To be naked"
always contains a suggestion of physical freedom and I would
eagerly convert myself to this harmony between hand and
flower, to this sensuous alliance between the earth and man
freed of humanity if it were not already my religion.

These passages have the intensity of a writer's most personal vision.
They stand behind Camus's entire work and reappear at the surface at
those moments when he speaks in his own voice: when Rieux and Tarrou
free themselves of the historical curse of the plague in a regenerative
plunge into the sea; when the snow falls on Amsterdam at the end of
Clamence's confession in *The Fall*. We can see from these passages that
what Camus calls solitude in the later notebooks is not, in fact, solitude
at all, but the intolerable intrusion of others upon the sacred moment
when man's only bond with reality is his bond with nature. In Camus's
mythology, the historical parallel to this moment is Greece and he
laments at length the disappearance from our own world of Hellenic
simplicity—as he laments the disappearance of landscapes from his own
books. He quotes Hegel: "Only the modern city offers the mind the
terrain in which it can be conscious of itself" and comments:
"Significant. This is the time of big cities. The world has been
amputated of a part of its truth, of what makes its permanence and its
equilibrium: nature, the sea, etc. There is consciousness only in city
streets!" And yet cities play an important part in Camus's novels: *The
Plague* and *The Fall* are intensely urban in spirit; Amsterdam and Oran
are far more than a mere backdrop; they play as central a part as any of
the characters. But in Camus's cities a man does not come to know
himself by contact with others even by experiencing the impossibility of
such contact. In their inhuman anonymity, they are the nostalgic

equivalent of the unspoiled nature that has departed from this earth. They have become the haven of our solitude, the link with a lost Arcadia. When city and nature unite in a landscape of nostalgia at the end of *The Fall*, his hero's outcry seems natural enough: "Oh sun, beaches and the isles under the seawind, memories of youth that cause one to despair!" Baudelaire knew a similar nostalgia in the midst of the modern city, but he set himself sharply apart from those who gave in to it, extending to them only pity. The *Notebooks* make it clear that, on this point, there is no distance between Camus and his fictional characters. And whereas the nostalgic figures in Baudelaire feel the attraction of a homeland that has really been theirs, Camus feels nostalgia for a moment that is ambivalent from the outset.

For if one considers this moment, to use his own words, as an instant of "physical freedom" when the body fits within the balance of the elements, then it would be a legitimate assertion of natural beauty on a rather primitive level. "The world is beautiful and nothing else matters." The sentence expresses an idyllic state that does not involve other people and stands outside time—Adam not only before the Fall but before the birth of Eve. In this condition "love is innocent and knows no object." Solitude is no burden since so little consciousness is present; on the contrary, it protects us from alien intrusions. One could compare the feeling with passages in D. H. Lawrence or understand in its terms Camus's affinity with certain aspects of the early Gide. It could be the basis for an amoral and asocial anarchism: Camus explicitly stresses that this encounter can only take place between nature "without man" and man "freed of humanity." This "nakedness" is an athletic freedom of the body, an Arcadian myth that the romantic neo-Hellenists could only have treated in an ironic mode. Camus's use of irony and ironic narrative devices never put this fundamental vision in doubt; in the privacy of his *Notebooks*, it asserts itself even more powerfully as an act of indestructible faith. Camus protests against history as a destroyer of nature and a threat to the body. History is a diabolical invention of German philosophers, a modern curse: "The whole effort of German thought has been to substitute for the notion of human nature that of human situation and hence to substitute history for God and modern tragedy for ancient equilibrium.... But like the Greeks I believe in nature." In this respect, Camus is indeed as remote as possible from existential modes of thought, and one can understand his irritation at being so frequently associated in people's minds with Sartre. In a remark that anticipates their future quarrel, Camus accuses Sartre of wanting to believe in a "universal idyll"—apparently unaware that he is himself the prisoner of an idyllic dream that differs from the one he attributes to Sartre only in the respect that it is personal rather than universal. There is no evidence that he ever woke up from this dream.

Camus's work, however, does not display a consistent development of this single vision. Even in the quoted passage from his earlier notebooks, when his naive Hellenism asserts itself in its purest form, a word play on the term *dénuement* introduces the other aspect of his thought. The "nakedness" implied by the *nu* in *dénuement* suggests the barrenness of a human condition that is essentially unsheltered and fragile—not man's "physical freedom" but his subservience to the laws of time and mortality. Camus has a sense of human contingency. The *Notebooks* record many brief episodes, imagined or observed, in which the frailty of the human condition is suddenly revealed when everyday routine is interrupted by an unexpected confrontation with death or suffering—as when he records his mother's horror at the thought of having to face the War years in the dark because of the blackout, or notes the expression on people's faces in a doctor's office, or tells of the death of an old actor. On a larger scale, the nightmarish aspects of the last War have the same effect, but several notebook entries reveal Camus's sensitivity to this kind of experience well before the war.

His best essay, *The Myth of Sisyphus*, develops from observations of this kind. His particular moral sense, one of protectiveness, is rooted in this awareness of man's "nakedness." But this nakedness has nothing in common with "physical freedom." A reconciliation of the two notions is not easily achieved; it comes about only in the highest manifestations of art or thought. And the first step in such a reconciliation always involves the renunciation of the naive belief in a harmony at the beginning of things. When Camus characterizes Greek art as a "benign barrenness" (*un dénuement souriant*), he does not seem to realize that this equilibrium is the final outcome, and not the starting point, of a development that is anything but "natural." Rooted in a literal and physical notion of unity, his own thought falls apart, on the one hand, in a seductive but irresponsible dream of physical well-being and, on the other, in a protective moralism that fails to understand the nature of evil. Camus never ceased to believe that he could shelter mankind from its own contingency merely by asserting the beauty of his own memories. He made this assertion first with proud defiance in *The Stranger*, and later, with more humility but no essential change, in *The Fall*. He always considered himself exemplary, the privileged possessor of a happiness the intrinsic quality of which he overestimated. Others, whose sense of happiness was deeper and clearer than his own, had long since understood that this gave them no increased power over their own destiny, let alone over that of others. His work contains some beautiful flights of lyrical elation along with some astute observations on the incongruity of the human condition. It is lacking however, in ethical profundity despite its recurrent claims to high moral seriousness. And it is entirely lacking in historical insight: ten years after its publication *The Rebel* now seems a very dated book. The *Notebooks* make the reasons for this failure clearer. Without the unifying surface of a controlled style to hide them, the contradictions are much more apparent than in the novels or the essays. The figure that emerges is attractive in its candor, but not authoritative in its thought.

When Camus was a young man, he used to be a goalkeeper for a student soccer team and he wrote articles, in the club paper, extolling the joys of victory or, even more eloquently, the melancholy of defeat. The goalkeeper of a soccer team is, to some extent, a favored figure: the color of his shirt differs from that of his teammates, he enjoys the privilege of touching the ball with his bands, etc. All this sets him apart from the others. But he has to pay for this by accepting severe restrictions: his function is purely defensive and protective, and his greatest glory to avoid defeat. He can never be the agent of real victory and, although he can display style and elegance, he is rarely in the thick of things. He is a man of flashy moments, not of sustained effort. And there is no sadder sight than that of a defeated goalkeeper stretched out on the field or rising to retrieve the ball from the nets, while the opposing attackers celebrate their triumph. The melancholy that reigns in the *Notebooks* reminds one of Camus's youthful sadness on the soccer field: too solitary to join the others up front, but not solitary enough to forego being a member of the team, he chose to be the goalkeeper of a society that was in the process of suffering a particularly painful historical defeat. One could hardly expect someone in that difficult position to give a lucid account of the game.

SERGE DOUBROVSKY

The Ethics of Albert Camus

For Sartre, Mauriac, and many others who may or may not have written, the deep shock felt, at Camus's death, combined with personal sorrow, is the feeling of a work suddenly stopped in full momentum, mutilated. As Malraux said long before, through Moreno in *Man's Hope*, "The capital thing about death is that it renders irremediable all that which has preceded it...." For the writer, however, all the effort of writing is directed, before death, at escaping death. The author dead, the work continues; it lives. It can not progress, but it can be enriched. It could not be modified, but through its relation to new minds it can be renewed....

During Camus's lifetime already, in order to neutralize his message, attempts were made to ossify his work, to disarm it by means of one or two often repeated epithets. At first, the word was "existentialism." Camus protested in vain on many occasions against the appellation and the affiliation, going so far as to attack by name the philosophy that was attributed to him: to no avail. One can still consult several manuals, especially the Anglo-Saxon ones; there lies Camus under the heading "existentialism." But this is not really troublesome; and existentialism is a scarecrow only for imbeciles. Although it is, in fact, an error in classification, it wrongs no one. More serious, is the stereotyped image: Camus, the moralist par excellence of the immoral

From *Critical Essays on Albert Camus*, Bettina L. Knapp, ed. © 1988 by Macmillan Library Reference. Originally published in *Preuves*, no. 116 (October 1960): 39–49. Translated by Sondra Mueller and Jean-Marc Vary. Reprinted by permission.

twentieth century; the austere, just, righteous preacher. We need only consult the obituary notices. Some congratulate him for it, others detest him for it. His will to be ethical, his moralism is praised or denounced: it is none the less an established fact. Some people do not hesitate to speak of "Jansenism" and Camus, like Racine's Phèdre, becomes a Christian without grace. Or again, Camus is not a believer and that is just the point: a professor of ethics, he knows only a professor's ethic, two or three abstract notions which he exalts. There again, in spite of his protestations, Camus had been witness to his metamorphosis. "Like everyone, I tried as best I could, to correct my nature by means of an ethic; that is, alas, what cost me most" (*L'Envers et l'endroit*).

Morality? What morality? That is what we should like to examine here. When re-reading Camus, we are struck by the repetition of a certain number of terms that seem to come out of a course on ethics: justice, happiness, revolt, etc. These words reoccur repeatedly, like a call to order, in the editorials of *Combat* and in the polemical exchanges with his contradictors. In his personal and philosophical essays they are constant themes of meditation, focal points of his thought. All Camus may seem to be contained in his choice of a particular glossary. Yet, and this is remarkable, these key words are never rigorously examined and really given a definition. It might be objected that the words "absurd" in *The Myth of Sisyphus*, "revolt" in *The Rebel*, are analyzed at length, and often in an authoritative way. But the analysis is, so to speak, horizontal rather than vertical, proceeding by extension rather than by inclusion. Revolt leads back to the original emergence of value, the emergence of value to the consciousness of evil, the consciousness of evil to the inverse affirmation of happiness and justice. But what of happiness, justice? The contents of these concepts, their immediate and far-reaching implications, the dialectic of inclusion or exclusion that relate them are all latent. Though Camus feels these concepts, he does not explore them in depth, in the sense that Sartre, for example, links his phenomenological descriptions of shame, fear, and anguish to a complete and rigorous view of man. In our opinion, the value of Camus's processes of thought derives from the very fact that they are lived rather than reasoned. "I am not a philosopher and I know how to speak only of what I have experienced" (*Actuelles II*). This does not mean, of course, that a philosopher must of necessity speak about what he has not experienced. But insofar as he integrates experience within a system, he transforms it. Dialectics gradually take the place of intuition.

Phenomenology is set in motion, truths must fall in and be arranged. In contrast, Camus has no system, no general framework, no philosophy. He grasps firmly only a few discontinuous truths which grip him: "I held on to truth as much as it held me" (*The Stranger*). We may as well get used to it. We can argue for and against, put in balance ... integrity and entirety, existence and philosophy, and raise all the problems of a philosophy of existence. This is what Jaspers did, and others besides. At any rate—and this is to the point—it is impossible to extract a "morality" from Camus's various intuitions and an "ethic" from his meditations on ethics. Camus's thought has been reproached both for its lack of practical application and for its excessive morality. But we may well question the notion of an ethic devoid of practical applications, an ethic, if ethic there be, defined as an ensemble of rules and precepts. What Camus's monotonous and powerful appeal to "justice" or to "happiness" reveals is in fact, an existentialist tension, rather than any rules for living. Above all, Camus is a poet, or to be more exact he has the sensitivity, the vision of a poet. But can a man innocently be a poet in our century? Insofar as Camus clothes his intuitions with reasoning, he distorts them.

"A man's work is nothing other than the long voyage to rediscover by the detours of art the two or three simple and great images which first gained access to his heart" (*L'Envers et l'endroit*, preface). All Camus's thought resides in a few elementary childhood experiences, in the way they "opened" him to the world. The famous "Mediterranean wisdom" with which he was so often taunted, is not, as was wrongly claimed, a luxury born of a bourgeois culture. As a child, and a child of illiterates, Camus, at the time of his fundamental experiences had not attained the realm of culture. He attempts rather, consciously and sometimes awkwardly, to recapture the *precultural* springs of existence. The fundamental existential experience that haunts Camus and which he tried to express through the lyrical descriptions in his first essays—works to which one must always return because they never ceased to be true for him—through the myths of the "Algerian race" and the "towns without pasts" (is there a writer who does not create his own myths?), in the last chapters of *The Rebel* in brief, is the world lived as heat and light, is the sun.

Sartre, in the analyses at the end of *Being and Nothingness*, has sufficiently emphasized the importance of the tangible in presenting immediate symbols for the interrelation of our consciousness and the world; in his "psychoanalysis"—to use Bachelard's word—of snow, of the viscous, etc. It is not surprising that no theoretical analysis of the solar can be found in Sartre since, after all, the sun seems absent from his personal universe. Or, to state matters more exactly, it plays a negative role: "I shan't do anything worthwhile, except perhaps, at nightfall. That's because of the sun ..." (*Nausea*). The redeeming virtues of night are defined in relation to the negated sun; it is because they are *anti-solar* that they give Roquentin a temporary respite from nausea. There is, of course, the disappearance of light ("Nausea remained down below, in the *yellow light*"), but what especially counts is the disappearance of heat: "I am happy: the cold is so pure, so pure tonight! Night leads back to cold, cold to purity. We follow the slope, the orientation of Roquentin's existentialist reverie: "Am I not myself a wave of chilled air? To have neither blood, nor lymph, nor flesh ... To be only a part of the cold." The sun is no longer "Noon the just" of Valéry's "Graveyard by the Sea," "Noon up there, motionless Noon," the plentitude of being against which the revolt of life must be affirmed: it is the *vital* force itself. Camus considers the sun in the same way as does Sartre, but only to oppose Sartre as he opposed Valéry. Camus's sun, unlike Valéry's, is not the manifestation of a spherical form of being, closed in on itself.... It is always the sun shining on the ruins of Tipasa, the sand beach of *The Stranger*, or the sea. It is light felt not as a distant purity, but as a fecundating bath. It is the unifying force of the cosmos: "From the earth to the sun a heady alcohol rises over the whole expanse of the earth, making heaven sway" (*Noces*). Gliding over all things, penetrating all things, overwhelming in its presence, the sun is the very symbol of that vital participation through which the realms of nature and of man are united: "Outside the *sun*, *kisses* and wild *perfumes*, all seems futile to us" (*Noces*).

The theme of the "sun," therefore, defines the fundamental category in Camus's ontology: participation. It is perhaps worth recalling here young Camus's vivid interest in Plotinus. His experience is the very opposite of Sartre's nausea. Sartrean "nausea" has its source in the double awareness of subject and object, of the absolute separation of consciousness and nature—in man's impotent negation of being as he tries symbolically to "reject" a world from which he is effectively rejected. With Sarte, we live a godless Cartesianism, whereas in Camus we detect a Bergsonism but without teleology. Though life in Camus's work no longer moves in an ascending and reassuring direction, it still has impetus; though it has lost its finality, it has preserved, so to speak, all its vitality. The body is the place where man and nature meet in a happy "marriage."

In the solar world of Camus, the muscular indolence and eurythmy of bodies reigns without contest. Animality is fully accepted. Camus is far from thinking in terms of self-enjoyment or of a hedonistic retreat within. ("To take pleasure in oneself is impossible." *L'Envers et l'endroit*, preface). The body is the privileged place of joy, because it is the locus of harmony, and union is in fact unison. Physical love places human beings against the background of Being, and participation in the act of love is the symbol of a deeper participation. Meursault feels his love for Marie while swimming: "The water was cold and I felt all the better for it. We swam a long way out, Marie and I, side by side, and it was pleasant to feel how our movements matched, hers and mine, and how we were both in the same mood, enjoying every movement." Nor is it by chance that Meursault's love for his mother, instead of being a latent and permanent sentiment, as required by psychological myths which are only disguised forms of morality, always wells up from sudden perception: "Through the rows of cypress trees ... that tawny brown and green earth ... I understood Mother." The spontaneous identification of earth and mother defines Meursault's "cybelian" [Cybele: goddess of the earth] mode of existence, plunging to the telluric sources of his being where in the words of the poet Claude Vigée, all love is "a happy incest."

It is easy to see how an ontology such as this can affect ethics. Vital participation is both act and value. We can mask fact for others and for ourselves, but a value will emerge precisely at the time of the unmasking. In this light it should be noted that at the end of *The Stranger*, Meursault's famous "awakening" and his accession to the ethical life do not arise out of the rejection of his past "animality," or of his physical mode of existence; of his adherence and adhesion to the moment, to the earth, given him in a succession of sensations; of his fidelity to the present and to presence in spite of all the attempts of society to create a continuous time and a logical world. On the contrary, the imminence of death makes explicit those values which heretofore had been implicit only. Meursault's life, suddenly limited and arrested, is not struck retrospectively with absurdity, as happens for Sartre's Pablo, in *The Wall*:

Death had disenchanted everything.... If, someone had come
to tell me that I could go home peacefully ... it would have
left me cold: a few hours or a few years of waiting, it's all the
same, when one has lost the illusion of being eternal. I was
anxious about nothing; in a sense, I was calm.

In contrast, Meursault says,

That meant, of course, I was to die. Also, whether I died now
or twenty years hence, this business of dying had to be got
through, inevitably. Still, what troubled me in my reasoning
was the terrible jump my heart gave at the thought of twenty
years of life yet to come.

Threatened with annihilation, life gathers and concentrates its force,
becomes conscious of itself and proclaims that it is the only value: "And
I, too, felt ready to start life all over again." Far from rendering life
absurd, death is the element which gives it its full meaning. Life retrieves
and reabsorbs death, and in its very defeat triumphs, since death which
denies life succeeds only in reaffirming life. In Cybele, Apollo and Hades
were reconciled:

In a few moments, I shall throw myself down among the
absinth plants letting their fragrance invade my body and, all
prejudices to the contrary, I shall know that I am fulfilling the
truth which is the truth of the sun and will also be that of my
death (Noces).

This, of course, suppresses neither the reality nor the horror of death.
For death is not manifest only at the end of a life, but at its very heart,
and then it is called suffering. With Meursault, the problem, in a sense,
was posed too simply, too neatly. His beautiful animality is to be
destroyed, but it is not impaired. He is going to die a lusty young man,
but he will not suffer in the flesh.

With The Plague, we move from death suffered in full health to
death suffered in illness. Pus mingles freely with the absinth plants of
Noces (Nuptials), which reappear at the end of The Stranger: "The cool
night air, veined with smells of earth and salt, fanned my cheeks. The

marvelous peace of the sleepbound summer flooded through me like a tide." Flesh does not perish only, it disintegrates. It does not disintegrate after death only, but in life. Life and death are not only opposed one to the other, they inter-penetrate. The problem becomes more painful and more complex, but it remains fundamentally unchanged. This is made clear in the significant episode toward the end of *The Plague*, the end of the long combat with Evil and the long conversation between Rieux and Tarrou, who from all this draws the lesson: "Do you know," he said, "what we ought to do for friendship's sake?" "Whatever you wish," said Rieux. "Take a dip in the sea; even for a future saint, it's a worthwhile pleasure." The friendship between the two men, like the love of Meursault and Marie, regains its essential truth in the contact with water, as the two men swim "in the same cadence": "For some minutes, they advanced with the same cadence and vigor, alone, far from the world, liberated at last from the city and the plague." The narrator had already spoken, at the beginning of the passage, of "the outer world which can always save everything ..." Rather than the stoic pronouncements he sometimes coined, this is the intuition which lies at the center of Camus's ethic.

If our analysis is accurate, it ought to help us get rid of two misunderstandings which weigh disastrously on the work and the person of Camus. First, the famous "heroism," to which we are told his message can be reduced. This error contains a share of truth, like all errors. The Tarrou side of Camus, in truth the temptation of heroism, is apparent in Camus's tendency to refuse emotion, in the kind of inflexibility with which he comes to grips with fate and which is often reflected in stiffness in his style, in his constant search for the concise phrase. "What interests me," says Tarrou with simplicity, "is to know how one becomes a saint." Evidently, Camus, too, is interested. But in his moments of weakness, when the demands he makes upon himself grow weak, Rieux, who, after all, is the narrator of the book and who survives whereas Tarrou dies, answers his friend, his alter ego: "I have no taste, I believe, for heroism and sainthood. What interests me is to be a man." "Yes, we are seeking the same thing, but I am *less ambitious*." One can easily understand why heroism is a facile solution, a least effort: as the characters of Malraux's *Man's Fate* show, heroism is essentially a turning in on oneself by a confrontation with death.... Camus moves in the opposite direction when at the end of *The Rebel*, he says that "in order to be a man" one must "refuse to be God"; when he breaks away from the ultimate ambition of heroism, it is because he is not thinking in terms of a closed, circular ethic; it is because all his thought tends to define an ethic of "openness" to the world and to others, an ethic of participation.

There is a certain form of participation that is called enjoyment. A propos of Camus, Gide has often been mentioned, and Camus has been taken to task for affinity with the apostle of hedonism, at a time when "commitment" was considered indispensable. Hedonism, too, is one of the temptations Camus faced (who does not have his own?) but it is incompatible with the fundamental direction of his thought, with his "existential project." "Self-enjoyment is impossible; I know it, in spite of the great talents I could have applied to it" (*L'Envers et l'endroit*, preface). Camus finds this hedonism impossible, not in the name of an abstract morality, but because it is the nature of the body, of the "body proper" as the philosophers would say, to turn toward the world and be in harmony with the world. Resemblances with Gide in vocabulary or thought—sensation, present moment, light, sun, landscapes, etc.—are only superficial....

There is no Gidian hedonism in Camus. Camus's faithfulness to ever-repeated fundamental experiences is quite opposed to Gide's variety of experiences. The fundamental paucity and poverty of Camus's imagery of nature contrast sharply with Gide's varied landscapes, with Gide's many sentimental wanderings through reality as flitting "from flower to flower, from one thing to another" (La Fontaine). Camus's imagery is always drawn from the ruins of Tipasa, sun on rock, or the Mediterranean, the sea. When removed from his element, visiting Prague or the Scandinavian countries, Camus becomes lost, bewildered. Whereas Gide experiences everything in the plural, Camus experiences things in the singular. His solar experience is one of destitution and denudation. His is a "proletarian" relationship to the world, the relationship of someone who has nothing and whose contact with objects is not expressed in terms of having. Camus's domain is *being*, and this returns us to our preceding analyses of the vital force. The only possession is a rejoicing which is a participation.

Since heroism and hedonism are rejected, more from an ontological point of view than an ethical one, or to put it otherwise, once the concept of possession in the form of domination of self or of the world is disqualified, there obviously remains a basic problem to be solved in Camus's thought: that of the relationships between being and doing. This is the very heart of the quarrel between Camus and existentialism, a quarrel that caused so much ink to flow over the last ten years. One can easily follow the evolution of Sartre from *Nausea* to *Red Gloves*: all ontological solutions are closed to thought. Where consciousness is the illness of being, where the "for-itself" exists only as a continuous opposition to the "in-itself," and where the aim of the human being underlying all others is to synthesize the two contradictory entities—in other words, where, as Malraux had already stressed in *Man's Fate*, man's dream is to be God, any position which seeks a solution in being is necessarily doomed to failure. "Bad faith," which all Sartre's work is there to uncover and track down in all its machinations, is nothing but man's desperate effort to give the consistency of being to his existence, *to make himself exist* through symbolic possession of the world, through other people's view of him, etc. From then on, man is a "useless passion." The concept of authentic action is opposed to the state of real transcendence of the "absurd." "A priori, life is senseless ... but it is up to you to give it a meaning" (*Existentialism is a Humanism*). The important word here is *give*. "Bad faith" can introduce itself in our way of "giving a meaning," in such a manner as to have this meaning remain intentional, symbolic. Meaning can be given to one's life through deeds alone, or more precisely through actions, that is to say, a manner of behaving which is not an end in itself (this would be falling into heroism, an attitude denounced in *The Flies*), but which aims at an objective transformation of the world. Since history is the actual medium in which man comes into contact with the world, the existentialist philosophy of action will be a philosophy of historic action, entirely oriented toward the *future*. Sartre: "Existentialism will never take man as an end, for a man is always in a state of formation" (*Existentialism is a Humanism*). De Beauvoir: "It is in the light of the future, which is the meaning and very substance of the act, that a choice will become possible" (*For an Ethic of Ambiguity*). Simone de Beauvoir herself draws the consequences of this attitude in the following statement: "Men of today will be sacrificed to those of tomorrow because the present appears as the 'facticity' that one must transcend toward freedom." In this respect, the whole purpose, the whole effort of Camus's philosophy is directed at shutting this door so dangerously left open on the sacrifice of the living to the men of the future and at reinstating the inalienable value of the present in opposition to the future.

"This argument accepts life as being the only necessary good ..." (*The Rebel*). The moral philosophies of Sartre and Camus are what one could call "unidimensional philosophies," the one basing itself completely on the idea of liberty, the other on that of life. It is not accidental that throughout this essay we have pursued the parallel, or rather that we have been pursued by this parallel between Sartre and Camus. A perpetual confrontation such as this—which faces us in our every thought and action—does no more than express the absolute need of our time to redefine itself completely. Malraux had already said, "The age of the fundamental is beginning again," and in spite of the complexity of the problems, the fundamental choices are simple. A philosophy of liberty directed exclusively toward action is a philosophy of abandon, of the radical separation of man and world, a philosophy in which the world becomes acceptable only when transformed by man. This explains the value given to the manufactured object in Sartre's work, the detailed analysis of the artifact and of all relations connected with the use of things, whereas, in contrast, Roquentin's "nausea" is triggered by the feel of a pebble on the beach. The dangers of such an existentialist attitude can easily be grasped: by denying itself communion through actual presence, it does away with the present in favor of the world transformed, "acted upon," i.e. the future. By cutting off humanity from being, by enclosing man in the humane and denying being to the human, it tends to upset the balance of existence leaving it in a false equilibrium, so to speak.

Philosophers like Merleau-Ponty have attempted to help man out of this dead end and to re-establish him on his ontological foundations. That is exactly what Camus does in the realm of ethics. To expect salvation to emerge from action is to postpone the justification of the action indefinitely, to perpetually refer to the problematical end of history. In her systematic effort to define an existentialist philosophy, Simone de Beauvoir was aware of the dangerous mirage inherent in the concept of distant goals: "The end justifies the means only if it remains present to us, if it is completely revealed during the enterprise itself" (*For an Ethic of Ambiguity*). However, because of the lack of a point of reference, of a permanent criterion, in short, of an absolute value, or, more exactly, because liberty is the only absolute value he possesses, the existentialist philosopher finds himself placed in a position forever oscillating between the end and the means: "One cannot judge the means without the end which gives it meaning, any more than one can detach the end from the means which define it." But from where then will the definition, the meaning, come? Under its humanized surface the world is absolute chaos. Man, we have been told, cannot be taken as an end since he is perpetually in the making. The refusal to take man himself as an end is all the more understandable since Sartre's theoretical analyses of our relationships to others as well as his literary investigation reveal that "hell is other people" and that for man "his number one enemy is man"; and this without our being able to blame any political system, since Sartre considers that it is an unchangeable ontological situation, a characteristic of man's condition and therefore impervious to any possible modification.

Freedom then remains as the supreme goal. But since freedom is a fact or if one wishes, facticity, as well as transcendency (we cannot not be free, we are *condemned* so to be), and therefore differs from a value that has yet to be, we can conceive of goals for freedom but not of freedom as a goal. For we cannot confuse liberty and liberation without being insincere. The chained slave is free as both the theoretician in *Being and Nothingness* and Orestes in *The Flies* know[1]; if he wants to be freed, it is because he wishes to find himself moving once again within the circuit of humanity; it is because he wishes to *live*.

Here we discern another value that liberty can no longer define. It is no longer possible to shut man up inside his own ipseity, to say with Simone de Beauvoir that man's problem consists in "pursuing the expansion of his existence and in recovering this very effort as an absolute." In a different manner, we have come back to the fruitless circularity of heroism. Human activity must open itself to the world, must surrender itself to the world and rediscover its natural source and dwelling, must live the experience of the sun. Simone de Beauvoir herself says this admirably well when she writes;

> To wish man free is to wish for being, it is to wish for the revelation of being in the joy of existence.... It is when our movement toward freedom takes on the consistency of pleasure, of happiness, that it assumes its real and palpable form in the world.... If we do not love life in our own selves and through our fellow man, it is useless to try to justify life.

This is exactly what Camus says throughout his work. But one can wonder how such an existential outlook is compatible with the existentialist attitude. How can the revelation of being be made through joy if the basic experience of being is expressed through "nausea"? How can one desire being and at the same time set up consciousness as the very negation of being? An orientation toward happiness, an unconditional love of life are indeed the concrete basis of all ethics, but then we need to change ontologies. What happened in fact was that the ethics of ambiguity surreptitiously passed from Sartre to Camus. And if in the last analysis we wish to give a concrete basis to moral philosophy, we must go back to the words of Camus: liberty opens upon life and the philosophy of existence upon the philosophy of being.

We now have before us one of these arresting Camus truths. The "yes" triumphs over the "no." "I came to realize that at the core of my revolt lay a consent.... How does one sanctify the union of love with revolt?" (*Noces*). But simultaneously an inverse reaction takes place: revolt exists side by side with consent: both find expression in an equilibrium of opposites. Therefore we have not reached one of those philosophical "principles" that would allow us tragically to "deduce" a philosophy, an axiom from which we could draw laws and precepts as in the good old days of rationalism. Hardly has the "yes" been posited before the "no" rises in opposition. "Man is the only creature that refuses to be what he is" (*The Rebel*). Horror and injustice exist within our own selves, in others, and in the world. Thus in a simultaneous "yes" and "no" Camus defines a dialectic of confrontation, of opposition, of anguish without transcendence. Camus's well-known "concept of limitations" simply means that an affirmation of life must be made which does not end in a complete negation of the world. Camus knew full well that to emphasize the "vital" was not without danger. Nietzsche had encountered the same problem only to fall into the "superman" trap and into the error of biological expansionism; we are well aware of what followed when these ideas were taken up by others. Life can be deadly; the sun kills, as Meursault finds out when he shoots the Arab without reason: "My eyes were blinded by a curtain of salty tears. I felt only the sun beating down relentlessly upon my forehead. The pure and simple submission to vital forces without the counterweight of moral revolt ends in the destruction of these forces; vitalism escapes nihilism only on the condition that life accept a sacrifice; it must cease to limit itself to the individual; it must transcend itself by moving into the realm of the universal: "Within the limits of the 'absurd' experience, suffering is individual. Starting with the movement of revolt, we are aware of suffering as a collective experience, as everyman's adventure. I revolt, therefore we are" (*The Rebel*). This defines the evolution of Camus's thought from *The Stranger* to *The Plague*.

A moral philosophy of action is thus superimposed upon—one might even say spans—a philosophy of being. This is the sensitive core, the touchstone of any doctrine today. Action in Camus's eyes must remain faithful to its twofold origin, the "no" sitting in judgment, and the "yes" ready to "change life but not the world." Divided at its source, action can only be charged with anguish. Since it no longer attempts to reach the absolute, which is found only on the level of being, it can only be imperfect. "Poverty prevented me from believing that all is well in history and in the world; the sun taught me that history is not everything." Camus has often been criticized for rejecting history because he did not accept it exclusively. The fact that he set it in a broader ontological context does not mean that he substituted the concept of history for something else. But at a time when history, in the case of many, has become the only dimension of the human drama, Camus refers us to something which underlies history and without which history could not exist.

In the course of the debate caused by *The Rebel*, Sartre criticized Camus for placing human values in "the battle of man against heaven" and by so doing forgetting the concrete and historical reasons for action. It is quite true that in a way *The Plague* presents a perfect situation in which all human beings can unite to fight the inhuman. But, after all, the book is also an allegory and must so be understood. It does not negate history, but extracts an ultimate meaning from it. If man habitually can and should (most of all, perhaps) fight man, it is insofar as man becomes a scourge and assumes the role of the plague. The oppressed says to the oppressor: "Get out of my sun." Action as conceived by Camus can never be satisfied with being a praxis; it is never a form of salvation in itself; it is never circular at any time. Though necessary, it is always deceptive, in fact somewhat mystifying if it is not rooted in the world of the present, in life itself. As Simone de Beauvoir so aptly said, "If the satisfaction of an old man drinking a glass of wine has no value, then production, wealth, are only empty myths. Man is not "the future of man"—to use the words of the poet Francis Ponge, so dear to the existentialists—he is man's present.

Immediate practical consequences stem from Camus's moral philosophy which some have described as being so ethereal: "I shall have pleaded my case ... so that *from this very moment* the agonizing pain of man be lessened" (*Actuelles*). No appeal to the realm of ends, of the future, can justify any attack on the present, on life which is an inalienable value. Camus squarely sets up an ethic of being in opposition to the ethics of action, and at this point he breaks with existentialism and Marxism. Camus never denied that in certain exceptional cases, the use of violence might be a weapon, but he always refused to accept that it might become a policy. A simple nuance perhaps, but for millions of human beings, one which is capital in importance. In this sense certainly, Camus was the conscience of our time, repeating in vain perhaps what Ionesco was to illustrate in his play *The Killer*: that we could not build the "shining city" in defiance of nature without immediately bringing the Killer into existence.

One might object that it is very easy to be a "conscience" and this obviously raises the whole problem of the "clean" and "dirty" hands having an equal chance of bringing some consolation. But, we ask, how does the evolution from *The Stranger* to *The Plague*, from the subjective to the "we are" attitude find its application on the practical level? Camus proposes an ontology; nevertheless a concrete ethic, in other words, a policy, still has to be defined, for it would be pointless to establish an "Algerian" ethic which would not begin by dealing with Algeria, for example. And how will the "yes" and "no" offset each other in this particular instance? "What we need is to define a modest policy, a policy just as free from any trace of Messianism as from the nostalgia of a Garden of Eden" (*Actuelles*). Will Camus's ethic of moderation then end up only in a policy of moderation? When Camus writes, "There is only one thing left for us to try, and that is honesty without illusion, a wise loyalty ...," this wisdom may seem limited and disappointing, but we must admit that there exists no ethical or political position that does not have its pitfalls. The pitfalls inherent in the concepts of absolutism in action or history are too obvious these days to require any comment. What Camus called the nihilism of efficiency at any cost has more than shown its inhuman consequences. But the opposite danger of abstention and inactivity is also present. It is a real danger and no formula exists which allows us to evade it. Both the middle of the road and the royal road can be fatal. The first, however, offers our civilization more chances of survival than the second, whose end we know only too well.

We shall not discuss those personal commitments or refusals to be committed which concern Camus alone. We merely note that, when necessary, Camus paid with his own person, and that his reticence very often coincided with a near withdrawal. But he never claimed that he was playing an exemplary role nor did he ever set himself up as a model. Passionately in search of an ethic, he never claimed he was a moralist. As his preface to *L'Envers et l'endroit* (Betwixt and Between) clearly shows, he was aware that he was fallible. The exponents of virtue who dream of being judges are dealt with in *The Fall*. To those who demand coherent, satisfying, and clearly stated policies—to systematic minds, to the organizers and administrators—we can only answer that Camus, like the most beautiful girl in the world, can give only what he possesses.

In contrast to the fundamental experience described in most contemporary philosophies, he had a certain happy experience of being which appeared basic to him: he passed it on to us. Around him and in history he sees the consequences of uprooting: he tells us about them. Camus, who is a thinker though not a philosopher, instinctively perceives certain truths. They had escaped minds dialectically better prepared than his own, but minds that did not know how to extract consequences from these truths or who did not wish to extract them. He recalls these consequences inexorably, monotonously. He rediscovers the values of life and happiness lost in the tumult and terrors of our age. He places happiness, that is to say, the reconciliation of man and nature, above ethics and simultaneously rectifies the indifference inherent in nature, his own nature, through an ethic: solitude exploding in the movement of the heart toward his fellow-man. "Rieux straightened up and said in a firm voice ... that there was no shame in preferring happiness.—Yes, said Rambert, but there may be shame in being happy all alone" (*The Plague*).

This is the existentialist tension in Camus's thought that no theoretical formulation, no dialectic process can resolve. Camus gives us only two ends of the chain which we must hold at any cost. In its authenticity, Camus's "moderation" is quite the antithesis of comfortable, mediocre moderation. It is a painful and perpetual effort. The true contact with being and with others is not given. It can only be conquered over the commonplace, over habit. The tenacious will to come to grips with the present is not easy to maintain when one knows just how easy it is to count on the future or the past for one's own justification. "Moderation" is the only way through which to live and adhere completely to life. Basically, the discontinuous intuitions powerfully restated by Camus, once elucidated, reveal less what we should do than *what we should not do*. One cannot be a hero, a pleasure seeker, or a judge, and this is the sense of Camus's opposition to Malraux, Gide, or Sartre.

Camus's work does not set up an ethic, but in a way it does propose "prolegomena to any future ethic." As Claude Bourdet said in the conclusion of an article "Camus and the problem of Clean Hands," "If the time should come when in spite of present ups and downs France turns toward socialism ... then the warnings of Camus against the degradation of revolution may be useful to those who will then be facing certain dangers ..." If we lose a certain relationship to being, existence founders. These are the "traps" detected, the warning cries, desperate at times, that Camus raises in our time, clarion calls of the poet echoing through a city of philosophers and rhetoricians. Lacking that logical coherence which so often is only superficial and illusory, the warnings, the cries, the call possess an internal cohesion born of an unshakable certainty. If it goes deeply enough, analysis uncovers not a mine of ideas but an outpouring, a vital spring. There we must take our arguments to be refreshed. It seems that for Camus this is what constitutes all ethics. It must be *existential* in the full sense of the word, or it does not exist, or it becomes an anti-philosophy dedicated to man's destruction. No formula, no effort of discursive thought can absolve us from recreating experience ourselves within ourselves. Human beings though interdependent stand alone. Today, this is a truth not easily acceptable. Camus is neither the man in the street nor the "organization man." He is the man in the sun, on the lone naked rock, who knows that once the plague has come he must reenter the city. It is he who said, "My human passions have never been 'against'," and who during the struggle and beyond it, never forgot the reasons to love. This sun, this knowledge mean little to empire builders or creators of systems. Nevertheless, should the era neglect them, it will rush to its doom, and man's fate will be sealed the day he forgets how to love in spite of evil and suffering— this creation without a creator.

NOTES

1. "*Jupiter*: If you dare pretend that you are free, then the freedom of the prisoner loaded down with chains in the corner of his cell will have to be vaunted as well as that of the crucified slave.—*Orestes*: Why not?"

S. BEYNON JOHN

Image and Symbol
in the Work of Albert Camus

In intellectual power, coherence, and originality Albert Camus may not be the equal of Jean-Paul Sartre—with whom he shares certain affinities—but he speaks of man's predicament in accents so humane and generous that he attracts the attention of all those who care for the quality of life in contemporary Europe. It is precisely the attention paid to the ideological content of Camus's writing—the sense of the absurd, the idea of revolt—that has tended to divert critics from the study of the creative process in his novels and plays. The great majority of essays and articles devoted to Camus have concentrated on the philosophical value or the political relevance of his ideas, while those critics who have addressed themselves to Camus as an imaginative writer have often done so in passing, restricting themselves to generalities about his style and indulging a robust appetite for literary affinities. The present essay is, therefore, an attempt to examine critically a specific, and admittedly limited, aspect of Camus's literary talent: his creation of symbols. The essay has no pretensions to being exhaustive even in this direction and will be confined to tracing the process by which two images—sun and sea—recur in this author's work and achieve symbolical force.

The range of Camus's imagery is fairly narrow and derives almost entirely from the central experience of his life, his encounter with nature along the North African littoral. This experience is described directly

From *Camus: A Collection of Critical Essays*, Germain Bree ed. Originally published in *French Studies*, IX, No. 1 (January, 1955), 42–53. © 1955 by *French Studies*. Reprinted by permission of Oxford University Press.

113

and personally in his formal essays: *L'Envers et l'endroit* (Betwixt and Between) (1937), *Noces* (Nuptials) (1938), and "Le Minotaure ou la Halte d'Oran" (1945). From these essays a distinct sensibility emerges, born of an essentially pagan experience of nature. One's awareness of this paganism does not have to wait upon an older Camus's confession of emotions "recollected in tranquility." The Algerian child was certainly father to the successful man of letters respectfully approached by the editors of reviews:

> ... je ne suis pas chrétien. Je suis né pauvre, sous un ciel heureux, dans une nature avec laquelle on sent un accord, non une hostilité. Je n'ai donc pas commencé par le déchirement, mais par la plénitude. Ensuite ... Mais je me sens un cœur grec.[1]

> ... I am not a Christian. I was born poor, beneath a happy sky, into a nature which inspires a feeling of harmony, not hostility. I did not begin in privation but in plenitude. Later ... But I feel I have a Greek heart.

In fact, the paganism breathes through Camus's earliest pages. He confesses nostalgia for the lost Greek virtues, especially that "insolent candor" which characterized their enjoyment of the senses. He sees even the palpable symbols of Christianity threatened by more primitive and more potent forces:

> La basilique Saint-Salsa est chrétienne, mais chaque fois qu'on regarde par une ouverture, c'est la mélodie du monde qui parvient jusqu'à nous ...

> The basilica of St. Salsa is Christian, but each time one looks out through some opening, the melody of the world reaches in to us.

For the youthful Camus nature is animated by the ancient divinities. He records the fact with an engaging, if somewhat self-conscious, directness when he refers, on the opening page of the same essay, to the "gods that speak in the sun." The mark of this paganism, naturally enough, is the intense life of the senses. If the incidence of his imagery is any guide, Camus's most sharply attuned senses are those of sight and smell. He conveys powerfully the acrid scent of wild herbs that catches at the throat and he distinguishes the cargoes of visiting ships by their smell; timber in the Norwegian vessels, oil in the German, wine in the coasters. Auditory images are few and mainly concerned with the cry of birds and the sigh of the wind. These sounds usually serve to emphasize the surrounding silence and loneliness. It is, however, visual images that predominate, especially those connected with the blinding sun. In this Algerian landscape, light is crude and exorbitant. Camus amasses images of light, and the final effect, in some passages, is to produce that shimmering surface common to Impressionist painting. In the steady accretion of visual images, Camus suggests admirably that slight distortion of vision which intense light sometimes produces in extremely hot and dry climates. He contrives this by including, in a series of visual images, one image that combines both reflection of light and the sense of motion, as the following passages exemplify:

> ... la mer cuirassée d'argent, le ciel bleu écru, les ruines couvertes de fleurs et *la lumière à gros bouillons* dans les amas de pierres.

> ... the silver-plated sea, the raw blue sky, the flower-covered ruins and *the great swirls of light* upon the heaps of stone.

and again:

> Du haut des plateaux, les hirondelles plongent dans d'immenses *cuves où l'air bouillonne*.

> From atop the plateaus, the swallows plunge into huge *cauldrons of seething air*.

This device is symptomatic of the way in which Camus exploits his verbal resources in order to convey how powerful is the impact of natural phenomena. This is no more than an accurate reflection of his own reactions, for he experiences a sort of vertiginous identification with nature. He describes how he feels himself to be assimilated into nature, annihilated by the elements whose vibrating life is everywhere present:

> Ce bain violent de soleil et de vent épuisait toutes mes forces de vie ... Bientôt, répandu aux quatre coins du monde, oublieux, oublié de moi-même, je suis ce vent et dans le vent, ces colonnes et cet arc, ces dalles, qui sentent chaud et ces montagnes pâles autour de la ville déserte. (*Noces*)

> The violent bath of sun and wind exhausted my life-strength. Now, spread out to the four corners of the world, forgetful, having forgotten myself, I have become the wind and, within the wind, the columns and arch here, the stone slabs smelling of the sun and the pale mountains set around the deserted city. (Nuptials)

There are even intense moments when he longs for this annihilation, for the cessation of conscious being. How enviable is the dense integrity of *things* when compared with the divided nature of man, with that "fissure of being" (to borrow from the existentialist vocabulary) which separates man from the rest of nature:

> Quelle tentation de s'identifier à ces pierres, de se confondre avec cet univers brûlant et impassible qui défie l'histoire et ses agitations. Cela, bien entendu, est vain. Mais il y a dans chaque homme un instinct profond qui n'est ni celui de la destruction, ni celui de la création. Il s'agit seulement de ne ressembler à rien. ("Le Minotaure")

> What a temptation to identify oneself with these stones, to mingle with this burning and impassive universe which defies history and its agitations. This, of course, is in vain. But there is in every man a deep instinct which is neither for destruction nor creation: wishing merely to be like nothing at all. ("The Minotaur")

It is within the context of this particular experience of nature that Camus's references to the sun and the sea need to be set. These images figure prominently in Camus's work because they are obviously the representative images of the type of landscape in which he was born and spent the formative years of his life. Moreover, in Camus's autobiographical essays "sun" and "sea" are frequently set in contexts which lend them emotional overtones that prefigure the symbolical significance they attain later, in his imaginative writing.

For example, in these essays, allusions to the sun constantly evoke a tonality of violence. Camus is assaulted and dazed by the sun, "abruti de soleil"; (stunned by the sun) he is permeated by it, a porous vessel receptive to its heat. The same sense of violence is suggested by Camus's use of the image "tourbillons de soleil" (swirls of sun), an image that recalls the characteristic whirling suns which dominate many of Van Gogh's paintings and refract something of the intensity of that artist's vision. Again, the author writes of "... la tête retentissante des cymbales du soleil" (his head reverberating from the cymbals of the sun) and thus fuses into one striking image the idea of a blinding reflection of light (as suggested by the metal of the cymbals), and the sense of a violent physical reaction like the pounding of blood in the ears, implied by the notion of "cymbals" as instruments of percussion. The area and significance of such an experience is extended by a comment that Camus makes in one of the essays:

> Mais être pur, c'est retrouver cette patrie de l'âme où devint sensible la parenté du monde, où les coups du sang rejoignent les pulsations violentes du soleil de deux heures. (*Noces*)

> But to be pure was to find once more that homeland of the soul where one's link with the world becomes perceptible, where the beating of the blood overtakes the violent pulsations of the two-o'clock sun. (Nuptials)

Nor are the images that define the sun restricted to those which suggest simple violence; occasionally, they reflect the sense of destruction. Hence, when the sun rains down its light on to the stony fields near Oran, it is described in a destructive image: "... le soleil allume d'aveuglants incendies" (the incendiary sun sets blinding fires). Then again, the sun is not infrequently associated with silence, that is to say, the absence or negation of specifically human activity. This is the case when Camus depicts the deserted sea off Algiers at midday, or the ruins at Djémila where the presence of the sun and the brooding silence of nature—intensified rather than broken by the passing wind—confirm the transience of man's achievement. The sun and the silence, in a sort of elemental union, preside over the empire of *things*, where man figures almost as an accident.

The sea features in these personal records as the constant solace, the source of refreshment in a burning climate. It is the arena of youth and hence, of life, in so far as life can be equated with youthful vigor and the beginnings of the sexual cycle. Each summer the sea welcomes "a fresh harvest of flower-like girls"; it is the scene of easy, animal joy, of the arrogant play of muscles. Even the fall of waves upon the shore evokes an erotic image, "... les premiers rochers que la mer suce avec un bruit de baisers" (the first rocks that the sea sucks with a kissing sound) and so, though more obliquely and remotely, suggests the sense of renewal. The waters of the sea, glimpsed at the turn of each street in Algiers, are a reminder of relief from the dust and the hot stone. The mineral landscape at Oran conveys the sense of the permanence of nature in its massive inertness ("une gangue pierreuse," [a stony paste]), but this permanence suggests death, as is evidenced in the image "ces ossements de la terre" (the earth's bony remains), whereas the sea ("une mer toujours égale," [an unchanging sea]) also conveys the notion of permanence but in the context of perpetual renewal.

In his personal narratives of his life in Algeria, therefore, Albert Camus gives to "sun" and "sea" respectively a distinct tonality and, if we now turn to his imaginative writing, we can examine the process by which they acquire a symbolical sense; achieve another dimension, in a word, while retaining marked affinities with that emotional experience with which they are associated in the essays. The importance that "sun" and "sea" achieve in this way can best be gauged, not from any mechanical count of the frequency with which they recur, but rather from the context in which they appear. Indeed, both images tend to emerge fully as symbols only in passages of great significance in the novels and plays. Situated in such passages, they represent the focal point of a symbolical event or situation. The overriding metaphysical intention of the author may also supply, in certain instances, a relevant criterion by which to judge the force of this imagery.

In general, one may say that physical relaxation and mental serenity are associated with evening and moonlight in Camus's work, while violent sensation and the impulse to destroy are related to the intense heat and light of a Mediterranean day.

Albert Camus's first novel, *The Stranger* (1942), crystallizes this tendency more precisely in a series of related acts and offers a striking example of the process by which the sun is transformed into a symbol. The decisive series of events in this novel begins when the central character, Meursault, accompanied by two acquaintances, Raymond and Masson, takes a walk along a beach near Algiers, after enjoying an early lunch. It is not quite midday but already the glare of the sun off the sea is described as unbearable. The three men walk steadily until they sight in the distance two Arabs with whom Raymond has already been involved on account of his maltreatment of a former Arab mistress. Raymond instructs his two companions on the roles they are to play in the event of an affray. The Arabs draw nearer, and it is at this point that Meursault observes: "Le sable surchauffé me semblait rouge maintenant" (The overheated sand now seemed red to me). In this phrase, an obvious physical reference to the intense light of the sun on the sand foreshadows, in a figurative sense, the violence that is to follow. The color of the sand under the sun's rays suggests the shedding of blood. A scuffle ensues with the Arabs in which Raymond and Masson are involved. Blows are exchanged and then Raymond's opponent produces a knife, wounding him in the arm and the mouth. Both Arabs then retreat cautiously behind the brandished knife, and, finally, take to their heels. While they retreat, the three Frenchmen remain stock-still, "cloués sous le soleil" (nailed to the spot by the sun). Masson and Meursault assist Raymond to return to the hut and Meursault agrees to explain what has happened to Masson's wife and his own mistress, Marie, both of whom had been left behind in the hut. In the meantime, Masson accompanies Raymond to a neighboring doctor where he receives treatment, returning to the hut shortly afterwards. On his return, Raymond insists upon "taking the air" and when Masson and Meursault, alarmed at the prospect of another fight, offer to accompany him, he flies into a rage. In spite of his outbursts, Meursault does in fact join him. They walk for some time along the beach, Meursault becoming increasingly aware of the overpowering sun which is reflected off the sand in dazzling splinters of light. The two men reach a tiny rivulet at the edge of the beach and find the two Arabs lying there, one absorbed in playing a monotonous tune on a reed pipe. The oppressiveness and fatality of the situation are suggested by references to the sun and the silence, while the faint sound of the stream and the notes of the pipe seem to express the potentialities, or at least the possibility, of life. Raymond, wishing to tackle his Arab antagonist on equal terms, hands his revolver to Meursault, who pockets it, but the Arabs scuttle away suddenly and a fight is averted. Raymond and Meursault return to the hut but Meursault, reluctant as ever to communicate with other human beings and dazed by the sun, does not enter the hut and returns along the beach for a solitary walk. In the course of this walk, the sun is described in terms of a hostile presence. It is as though the weight of the sun obstructs Meursault's progress, and the heat that emanates from it makes his body tense aggressively, as against a powerful assailant. The image employed here by Camus to describe the reflections of light, "chaque épée de lumière" (each rapier of light), suggests precisely the hostile nature of the sun. Meursault longs for shade and sees ahead of him the rock behind which the Arabs had disappeared. Striding towards it, he realizes with surprise that Raymond's attacker is lying there alone. The encounter between these two men now becomes the central point of a complex of images of light, so that the sun and the impulse to violence are invariably associated. The destructive act takes place under the aegis of the sun and seems to be a simple extension of its influence. The shape of the Arab dances before Meursault's eyes in the flaming air and the sea is like molten metal. It is at this point that the possibility of human initiative is suggested, but the sun overwhelms the human will:

> J'ai pensé que je n'avais qu'un demi-tour à faire et ce serait fini. Mais toute une plage vibrante de soleil se pressait derrière moi.

> I thought then that all I need do was to turn back and it would all be over. But behind me a whole beach vibrating with sun was pressing down upon me.

Such a sun recalls to Meursault the heat on the day of his mother's funeral and this allusion further emphasizes the association between death and the sun. The blood pounds in Meursault's veins. The foci of light multiply; first, a flash from the blade of the knife which the Arab has drawn ("La lumière a giclé sur l'acier et c'était comme une longue lame étince-lante qui m'atteignait au front," [The light splashed out on the steel and it was like a long glittering blade striking me on the forehead]); next, the blur of light through the beads of sweat that tremble on Meursault's eyelashes and fall across his vision like a mist; and then again, the glitter of the blade, the reflection from which painfully probes the eyes. The world spins; fire seems to rain out of the sky. Meursault aims the fatal shots.

It will be seen how the sun, in its direct or indirect manifestations, provides a sort of baleful focus for these three related episodes and how the incidence of images of light increases as the events reach their destructive climax. The sun, experienced with such pagan receptivity in the early essays, again dominates these passages of *The Stranger* and unifies them insofar as it symbolizes violence and destruction. The key to this symbolical use of the sun lies in the metaphysical intention that animates Camus's work. The entire novel is an allegory of that absurd universe which Camus had described elsewhere—*The Myth of Sisyphus* (1942)—in philosophical terms. Meursault is the symbol of man perpetually estranged in the world and this conception is reinforced when Camus, lending the sun this potent destructive influence, absolves man from responsibility—hence from guilt—by reducing him to something less than man, to the status of an irresponsible element in nature. In this way, the notion of the absurdity of life, which is the central and governing irony of so much of what Camus has written, is underlined and given dramatic color.

In Camus's play, *The Misunderstanding*, produced in 1944, the sun is again used, though more obliquely, as a symbol of destruction. The play is another extended allegory on the absurd universe, and its dramatic tension is derived from the same irony. A mother and daughter (Martha) who keep an inn in a remote corner of Czechoslovakia murder rich travellers who lodge with them. The son of the house (Jan), who had left home to seek his fortune, returns many years later as a wealthy man bringing with him his wife (Maria) and their child. He presents himself at the inn without disclosing his identity and his mother and sister fail to recognize him. He takes a room; he is drugged and his inert body dragged to the river and thrown in, at dead of night. His wife comes in search of him the following day and reveals his identity. Martha discloses the happenings of the night but, instead of offering contrition or consolation to the distraught widow, she gives expression to the tragic irony of the situation:

> MARTHA ... Mais je ne puis mourir en vous laissant l'idée que vous avez raison, que l'amour n'est pas vain et que ceci est un accident. Car c'est maintenant que nous sommes dans l'ordre. Il faut vous en persuader.
> MARIA Quel ordre?
> MARTHA Celui où personne n'est jamais reconnu.

> MARTHA ... But I cannot die leaving you with the illusion that you are right, that love is not futile and that this is an accident. It's now that we are in the normal order of things. Of this you must be persuaded.
> MARIA What order?
> MARTHA The one where no one is ever recognized.

This is a clear metaphysical irony, but the motive which impels the two women to murder—even if intended figuratively—is oddly banal. It is the need to amass enough money, out of the pockets of their victims, to escape to an easier and more carefree existence close to the sea, in a warmer climate. It is in relation to these aspirations that the sun again emerges as a symbol of fatality and destruction, for the land to which Martha longs to escape is represented only by the sun and the sea. These two symbols recur several times in her thinking and lure her on to new acts of murder. It is, however, significant that the goal of Martha's dreams is symbolized by the sea inasmuch as it holds out liberty (from toil, from the asperities of her native climate), but by the sun in the degree to which it offers dark oblivion for her past activities. Hence, the Mother, when referring to this distant haven, suggests that there "... le soleil dévorait tout" (the sun devoured everything). Martha ardently approves:

> MARTHA J'ai lu dans un livre qu'il mangeait jusqu'aux âmes, et qu'il faisait des corps resplendissants, mais vidés par l'intérieur.
> LA MÈRE Et c'est cela, Martha, qui te fait rêver?

MARTHA Oui, car j'en ai assez de porter toujours mon
âme et fai hâte de trouver ce pays où le soleil tue les
questions. Ma demeure n'est pas ici.

MARTHA I read in a book that it devours even people's
souls and gives them bodies that glow but have nothing left
inside.
THE MOTHER And is that what you long for, Martha?
MARTHA Yes, I'm tired of always carrying around my
soul and I'm in a great hurry to find that country where the
sun silences all questions. I don't belong here.

The sun, in a word, burns in Martha's mind, lighting the way to
destruction. It is doubly destructive: first, in that it can only be enjoyed
over the corpses of Martha's victims, and next, in that the coveted power
it radiates annihilates conscience and thought and so voids man of his
humanity.

There occurs in Camus's work a disparity, or at least an unresolved
tension, between his literary sensibility and his philosophical ambitions,
especially as crystallized in *The Rebel* (1951), a study which integrates
and develops a number of themes previously introduced into Camus's
work. *The Rebel* attempts to create a sort of classical point of equilibrium
to which it will be relevant to refer problems of action and change in the
contemporary world. It seems to be dedicated to an aphorism that
occurs in the play, *State of Siege*: "there is no justice, but there are limits."
In fact, in its insistence upon restraint, limit and moderation, the spirit
of *The Rebel* is at variance with Camus's normal mode of feeling, which
is impassioned and intensely subjective. Camus's most natural manner of
expression (already evident in his early essays) is lyrical, by which I mean
highly personal and emotive, and this feeling passes over into his prose-
technique, creating poetic overtones that derive, partly from the
richness of his imagery, partly from his feeling for the rhythm and music
of a phrase. It is true that what I conceive of as Camus's authentic
manner is sometimes deliberately concealed. Thus, the prose style of
The Stranger which is clipped and laconic, reflects the deliberate
subordination of Camus's natural lyricism to the exigencies of his theme,
that of conveying the sense of the absurd. In the same way, much of his
novel, *The Plague*, is written in a rather dry and meticulous prose,

admirably suited to the ironical intentions of the author. Even so, in both these novels a distinct lyricism continues to vibrate below the surface, often erupting in passages of genuine poetic force, especially when Camus introduces an elegiac note. The language of the plays, on the other hand, is often unrestrainedly lyrical. Indeed, there are moments, particularly in *State of Siege* and *The Just Assassins*, where lyricism passes into an inflated rhetoric which weakens the author's achievement. If I have dealt with this at some length, it is to suggest the element of neo-Romanticism that exists in Camus's writing and which is underlined by the recurrence of the figure of the Romantic rebel in his plays—Caligula and Ivan Kaliayev, for example—and by his tendency to exalt the life of the senses. It is in the light of this literary sensibility that Camus's use of sea symbolism needs to be considered. At this point it will be useful to recall what a distinguished contemporary poet recently wrote about the imagery of the sea and the desert in Romantic literature:

> As places of freedom and solitude the sea and the desert
> are symbolically the same. In other respects, however, they
> are opposites. For example the desert is the dried-up place,
> i.e., the place where life has ended, the Omega of temporal
> existence ... The sea, on the other hand, is the Alpha of
> existence, the symbol of potentiality.[2]

Camus therefore approaches conventional Romantic usage of the sea in the symbolism of freedom which he associates with it, but he differs from many of the Romantic writers who used it as a literary symbol divorced from their own experience. Camus turns to the sea for a symbol because it is for him an intensely lived experience.

In *The Stranger* sea-bathing is one of the main delights of the clerk, Meursault. The sea is the scene of his first tentative caresses of Marie; it is a source of intense physical pleasure. As the action of the novel unfolds, however, the sea ceases to be merely a place where physical restraint disappears. To Meursault, awaiting trial in prison, the sea is identified with his longing for freedom. He associates the condition of being free with the sea, and the pleasures it offers—the motion of running down to the sea, the sound of the waves, the sensation of his body slipping into the water. The sea thus becomes the symbol of freedom as contrasted with the confining walls of his prison-cell.

In *The Plague* one of the consequences of the epidemic is the closing of the beaches and bathing pools of Oran. Maritime traffic ceases completely and the port is deserted, cordoned-off by military pickets. Hence, although the sea is there, it exists in the background and, as the plague increases in severity, the presence of the sea becomes less and less real in the minds of the inhabitants of the town. In the early weeks, the sea continues to have a real existence for them since it serves as a palpable reminder of a link with that outside world with which they are confident of resuming contact in the near future. But, as the plague establishes itself in all its terrifying permanence, the sea recedes from minds that no longer dare to dwell on freedom and are simply concerned to survive within the imprisoning walls of the town. As a symbol of freedom, the sea diminishes in reality as the action of the novel proceeds. That is why one of the later episodes of *The Plague* seems peculiarly significant. Dr. Rieux, accompanied by one of his voluntary assistants, Tarrou, concludes an exhausting day by a visit to one of his regular patients, an old man suffering from chronic asthma. They pass from the sick-room up to a terrace on the roof. It is November; the evening air is mild, the sky clear and brilliant with stars. In this atmosphere of serenity, Tarrou is moved to give Rieux an explanation of his motives for joining the voluntary organization created to combat the epidemic and, further, to reveal something of his personality, his principles and his aspirations, which he defines as the attempt to become a saint without God. This long personal confession creates new bonds of intimacy, mutual sympathy and respect between the two men and, at this point, Tarrou suggests that a bath in the sea would be a fitting pledge of their friendship. Rieux instantly agrees and they make for the port, gaining access to the quayside by virtue of their special passes. Here, for the first time in many months, they become really aware of the shifting presence of the sea. They plunge into the water and strike out together with regular, matching strokes. They feel themselves to be at last "... solitaires, loin du monde, libérés enfin de la ville et de la peste" (alone, far from the world, at last free of the city and the plague). The swim ended, they return to the town, full of a strange and secret happiness and ready to resume the fight against the epidemic. It is impossible not to feel that this episode has the character of a symbolical ritual. The plunge into the sea is at once an act of purification from the plague (insofar as the epidemic represents suffering, evil and death), a rite of friendship, and a means of recovering freedom or, at least, of being recalled to it. In this last sense, the sea might be said to reassert itself as a symbol of freedom for these two men, to imbue them again with the need to be free. The sea that has been hidden, remote and ineffectual, suddenly becomes actual and effective as a symbol of freedom in the heart of a city subjected to the arbitrariness and the brute determinism of the plague.

In no work of Camus's is the symbolical nature of the sea made more explicit than in his play, *State of Siege* (1948). In spite of the author's cautionary preface, this play has obvious and striking affinities with the novel, *The Plague*, and, like the novel, it can be interpreted at more than one level. It is a metaphysical play whose symbols relate to the eternal predicament of man in the face of evil and death. It may be read as a symbolical account of an enemy occupation in time of war or as a more general protest against totalitarian systems. The arrival of the plague in the town of Cadiz is presaged by the alarming passage of a comet which temporarily disturbs a people ridden with habit and inertia, and represented by a Chorus. The inhabitants quickly recover their composure and the Chorus expresses its jubilation for the sensual joy of living and for the bounty of the earth. In this genial atmosphere, the lovers, Diégo and Victoria, are revealed sharing a moment of blissful happiness. To crown the festive spirit, a troupe of actors begins its performance of a comedy in the main square. The Governor of the city arrives and addresses the citizens in terms that condemn the spirit of change and eloquently defend the principle of total stagnation. It is at this juncture that the plague strikes down its first victim, one of the actors. Doctors diagnose the plague and provoke panic in all classes. The Governor, after feeble attempts to mask the reality of the situation and to maintain the status quo, concludes a dishonorable bargain with the plague itself, incarnated in a sort of barrack-square martinet who demands the surrender of the city. Aided by a chilling female Secretary and by some members of the existing order, the Plague issues his edicts. These impose a series of totalitarian measures upon the people of Cadiz and, as their scope becomes clear to the citizens, they attempt to quit the city before all the gates are closed. It is at this critical stage in the action that the Chorus gives expression to the people's urgent desire for freedom in words which unmistakeably envisage the sea as the source and symbol of freedom:

Nous sommes les fils de la mer. C'est là-bas, c'est là-bas qu'il nous faut arriver ... Courons à la rencontre du vent. A la mer! La mer enfin, la mer libre, l'eau qui lave, le vent qui affranchit!

We are the sons of the sea. It's out there, out there that we must go ... We must run to meet the wind. To the sea! The sea at last, the open sea, the water that cleanses, the wind that liberates!

This symbolism recurs in the second part of *State of Siege*. This section of the play is dominated, first by a mordant satire on totalitarian bureaucracy, and next, by the fate of Diégo who is defeated by fear in his first challenge to the power of the plague but returns to the attack. In his second encounter, Diégo discovers that the plague is powerless against men who have lost their fear and accepted their "sacred duty" of revolt. He turns to one of the townsfolk who has been gagged as part of the policy of the plague and removes his gag. There is a moment of tense silence before the released man speaks, turning his head skywards in an attitude of interrogation. The sky gradually grows lighter and a breath of wind stirs the curtains of a windless city. It is the wind from the sea and, because it comes off the sea, the harbinger of freedom. This symbolical event supplies the dramatic climax of the play's second part. The final section of *State of Siege* records the desperate tactics employed by the Plague to undermine Diégo's initial victory. The issue remains in doubt for some time, but, when Diégo agrees to forfeit his own life so as to revive the stricken Victoria, his act of abnegation accomplishes the final defeat of the Plague. Not even the ironical entry of the Governor and his clique, symbolizing the return of a corrupt and reactionary order, quite invalidates Diégo's sacrifice. Their return, however, provokes a final spasm of hatred and contempt from Nada, a curious figure who represents—as is suggested by the punning Spanish name he bears—the spirit of nihilism. In a last spasm of negation, he throws himself into the sea and his mortal struggle there is reported by a fisherman in the play's concluding passage. It is surely significant that in these closing lines the sea should be depicted as a sort of live, raging creature devouring an enemy of human freedom, and that it should be apostrophized as the symbol of men in revolt—"O vague, ô mer, patrie des insurgés, voici ton peuple qui ne cédra jamais" (Oh tide, oh sea, home of rebels, these are your people who never yield)—men, that is, exercising their freedom.

In conclusion, we may say that when Camus particularizes, when he has his eye fixed *on the object* with a sort of innocent stare, then his images are fresh and telling—for instance, the imagery of fruit he employs to suggest the passing seasons in a choral speech of the play *State of Siege*. When, however, he reaches beyond the level of sense experience, he is less successful in bringing about that fusion of "disparate elements" which so often distinguishes new and memorable imagery. There is nothing remarkable about the choice of "sun" and "sea" as the respective symbols of destruction and freedom; indeed, in the case of "sea," I have suggested the exact contrary. Yet, both symbols grow so naturally out of a personal and vividly felt experience of nature that they remain free of the deliberate and rather artificial air they sometimes wear in the work of other writers. They retain an afterglow, as it were, of the intense pantheism which informed Camus's first physical encounter with them, and this lends them a relevance, an inevitability and, an impressiveness they might otherwise have lacked.

Notes

1. Interview originally published by Émile Simon in the *Reine du Caire* (1948) and reprinted in Albert Camus, *Actuelles. Chroniques 1944–1948* (Paris: Gallimard, 1950), p. 225.

2. W. H. Auden, *The Enchafèd Flood or The Romantic Iconography of the Sea* (London: Faber and Faber, 1951), p. 27.

Chronology

1913	Born in Algeria, November 7, 1913.
1914	Father drafted to fight in WWI and killed in France in September. Mother moves to Belcourt quarter of Algiers.
1918	Begins public elementary school.
1923	Obtains scholarship to attend the *lycée*.
1930	First tuberculosis attack.
1933	Camus registers as a student at the University of Algiers, and pursues a degree in philosophy. Grenier publishes *Les Illes*. In Germany, Hitler comes to power.
1934	Marries Simone Hié. Joins the Communist Party.
1935	Divorces Simone Hié. Establishes the *Thèâtre du Travail*. Begins *L'Envers et l'endroit*. Completes thesis, *Métaphysique chrétienne et Neôplatonism*, Christian Metaphysics and Neoplatonism, receives *Diplome d'Etudes Superieurs*.
1936	Spanish Civil War begins. Breaks with the Communist Party.
1937	Works on *Alger-Républicain* with Pascal Pia.
1939	Writes a series of articles on poverty in Kabylia. Volunteers for service in WWII, but is rejected because of his tuberculosis. Germany invades France.

1940	Moves to Paris. Completes *L'Etranger*. Marries Francine Faure.
1941	Returns to Oran; works as a teacher. Completes *Le Mythe de Sisyphe*.
1942	Severe attack of tuberculosis. Returns to France. *L'Etranger* is published. Begins *La Peste*. Joins the Resistance as an editor of *Combat*. Begins working as a reader/editor at Gallimard.
1943	*Le Mythe de Sisyphe* is published. Meets Jean-Paul Sartre. Meets Maria Casarès.
1944	*Les Malentendus* is staged in Paris at *Thèâtre des Mathurins*. Paris is liberated.
1945	*Caligula* is produced at the *Thèâtre Hébertot*.
1946	Begins editing *L'Espoir* series at Gallimard, which publishes major works by Simone Weil. Visits the United States.
1947	Leaves *Combat*. *La Peste* is published. French colonial uprisings in Madagascar and Algeria. French-Indo china war begins.
1948	*L'Etate de siège* staged in Paris at the *Thèâtre Marigny*.
1949	Appeals for clemency for Greek communists condemned to death. *Les Juste* is staged in Paris at the *Thèâtre Hébertot*. Visits South America. Long bout of tuberculosis begins.
1951	*L'Homme Révolté, The Rebel*, is published.
1952	Attacked in *Les Temps Moderne*. Breaks with Sartre. Resigns from UNESCO protesting Spain's admission.
1953	Assumes directorship of the *Festival d'Art Dramatique* in Angers. Francine becomes distraught at their marriage to the point of emotional illness.
1954	*L'Ete* is published.
1955	Publishes a series of articles in *L'Express* regarding the French-Algerian colonial conflict.
1956	*La Chute* is published. Visits Algiers, appeals for truce. His adaptation of Faulkner's Requiem for a Nun is staged at the *Thèâtre des Mathurins*. Protests the Soviet invasion of Hungary.

1957	Awarded Nobel Prize for Literature. Publishes *L'Exil et le royaume, Exile and the Kingdom.*
1958	Suffers episodes of suffocation and semi-asphyxiation from effects of tuberculosis.
1959	*Les Possédés*, his adaptation of Doestoevsky's novel *The Possessed* is staged in Paris at the *Thèâtre Antoine.*
1960	Is killed in an automobile accident January 4, from Lourmarin on the way to Paris.
1995	*Le Premier Homme*, the novel he was working on at the time of his death is published as edited by his daughter, Catherine.

Works by Albert Camus

Révolte dans les Asturies, a play by Camus and members of the *Thèâtre du Travail* (1936).

L'Envers et l'endroit, essay (1937); translated as as "Betwixt and Between" in *Lyrical and Critical* (1967); translated as "The Wrong Side and the Right Side" in *Lyrical and Critical Essays* (1968).

Noces, essays (1939); translated as "Nuptials" in *Lyrical and Critical* (1967); and in *Lyrical and Critical Essays* (1968).

L'Etranger, novel (1942); translated by Stuart Gilbert as *The Outsider* (1946); as *The Stranger* (1946); translated by Matthew Ward as *The Stranger* (1988).

Le Mythe de Sisyphe, philosophical essay (1942); translated by Justin O'Brien as *The Myth of Sisyphus* (1955) and in *The Myth of Sisyphus and Other Essays* (1955).

Le Malentendus suive de Caligula, plays (1944); translated by Stuart Gilbert as *Caligula and Cross Purpose* (1947).

Lettres à un ami allemand, political essays (1945); translated as "Letters to a German Friend," in *Resistance, Rebellion, and Death* (1961).

La Peste, novel (1947) translated by Stuart Gilbert as *The Plague* (1948).

L'Etat de siège, play (1948); translated by Stuart Gilbert as *State of Siege* in *Caligula and Three Other Plays* (1958).

Actuelles: Chroniques, essays and journalism (1950); parts translated in *Resistance, Rebellion, and Death* (1961).

Les Justes, play (1951); translated by Stuart Gilbert as *The Just Assassins* in *Caligula and Three Other Plays* (1958).

L'Homme Révolté, philosophical essay (1951); translated by Anthony Bower as *The Rebel* (1954).

Actuelles II: Chroniques 1948–1953 (1953); translated in part in *The Myth of Sisyphus and Other Essays* (1955) and in *Resistance, Rebellion, and Death* (1961).

L'Eté, essay; translated as "Summer" in *Lyrical and Critical* (1967).

Requiem pour une nonne, play adapted from William Faulkner's novel (1956).

L'Exile et le royaume, essays (1957) translated by Justin O'Brien as *Exile and the Kingdom* (1958).

Reflexion sur la peine capitale, by Camus and Arthur Koestler (1957); Camus's essay translated by Richard Howard as *Reflection on the Guillotine: An Essay on Capital Punishment* (1959).

Actuelles III: Chroniques algérienne, essays and journalism (1958); translated in part in *Resistance, Rebellion, and Death* (1961).

Discours de Suéde (1958); translated by Justin O'Brien as *Speech of Acceptance upon the Award of the Nobel Prize for Literature, Delivered in Stockholm on the Tenth of December, Nineteen hundred and Fifty-seven* (1958).

La Possédés, play adapted from Dostoevsky's novel *The Possessed* (1959) translated by Justin O'Brien as *The Possessed* (1960).

Resistance, Rebellion, and Death, essays translated by Justin O'Brien (1961).

Carnets, mai 1935–février 1942 (1962) translated by Philip Thody as *Carnets* (1963) and as *Notebooks, 1935–1942* (1963).

Carnets, janvier 1942–mars 1951 (1964) translated by Justin O'Brien as *Notebooks, 1942–1951* (1964) and by Philip Thody as *Carnets, 1942–1951* (1965).

Essais (1965).

La Mort heureuse, Cahier Albert Camus, no. 1, novel (1971) ; translated by Richard Howard as *A Happy Death* (1972).

Le Premier Camus, suivi de Ecrits de jeunesse d'Albert Camus, Cahiers Albert Camus, no. 2 (1973); translated by Ellen Conroy Kennedy as *Youthful Writings* (1977).

Fragments d'un combat: 1938–1940, Alger Républicain, Le Soir Républicain, edited by Jacqueline Lévi Valensi and André Abbou, 2 vols. (1978).

Journaux de Voyage (1978); translated by Hugh Levick as *American Journals* (1987).

Le Premier homme, novel, edited by Catherine Camus (1995).

Works about Albert Camus

Bloom, Harold, ed. *Albert Camus*. Modern Critical Views Series. New York: Chelsea House Publishers, 1989.

Bree, Germaine. *Camus*. New York: Harcourt, Brace, and World, 1964.

————. *Camus and Sartre*. New York: Dell Publishing Co. 1972.

————, ed. *Camus: A Collection of Critical Essays*. Englewood Cliffs, NJ: Prentice-Hall, Inc., 1962.

Bronner, Stephen Eric. *Camus: Portrait of a Moralist*. Minneapolis: University of Minnesota Press, 1999.

Freeman, E. *The Theatre of Albert Camus: A Critical Study*. London: Methuen & Co. Ltd., 1971.

Kellman, Steven G. *The Plague: Fiction and Resistance*. Twayne's Masterwork Series. New York: Twayne Publishers, 1993.

Knapp, Bettina L. *Critical Essays on Albert Camus*. Critical Essays on World Literature Series. Boston: G. K. Hall & Co., 1988.

Lottman, Herbert R. *Albert Camus: A Biography*. New York: Doubleday & Co., 1979.

Luppe, Robert de. *Albert Camus*. tr. John Cumming and J. Hargreaves. New York: Funk & Wagnalls, 1966.

Mairowitz, David Zane and Alain Korkos. *Introducing Camus*. Cambridge: Icon Books Ltd., 1996.

Maquet, Albert. *Albert Camus: The Invincible Summer*. tr. Herma Briffault. New York: George Braziller, 1958.

McCarthy, Patrick. *Albert Camus: A Critical Study of His Life and Work*. London: Hamish Hamilton Ltd, 1982.

Onimus, Jean. *Albert Camus and Christianity*. tr. Emmet Parker. University: University of Alabama Press, 1970.

Parker, Emmet. *Albert Camus: The Artist in the Arena*. Madison: University of Wisconsin Press, 1965.

Rhein, Phillip H. *Albert Camus: Revised Edition*. Twayne's World Authors Series. Boston: Twayne Publishers, 1989.

Rizzuto, Anthony. *Camus: Love and Sexuality*. Gainesville: University Press of Florida, 1998.

Showalter Jr., English. *Exiles and Strangers: A Reading of Camus's Exile and the Kingdom*. Columbus: Ohio State University Press, 1984.

Sprintzen, David. *Camus: A Critical Examination*. Philadelphia: Temple University Press, 1988.

Suther, Judith D. *Essays on Camus's Exile and the Kingdom*. University: Romance Monographs, Inc., 1981.

Tarrow, Susan. *Exile from the Kingdom: A Political Rereading of Albert Camus*. University: University of Alabama Press, 1985.

Thody, Philip. *Albert Camus*. MacMillan Modern Novelists Series. London: MacMillan, Publishers Ltd., 1989.

———. *Albert Camus: A Study of His Work*. London: Hamish Hamilton Ltd., 1957.

Todd, Olivier. *Albert Camus: A Life*. tr. Benjamin Ivry. New York: Alfred A. Knopf, Inc., 1997.

Vulor, Ena C. *Colonial and Anti-Colonial Discourses: Albert Camus and Algeria*. Lanham: University Press of America, Inc., 2000.

Contributors

HAROLD BLOOM is Sterling Professor of the Humanities at Yale University and Henry W. and Albert A. Berg Professor of English at the New York University Graduate School. He is the author of over 20 books, including *Shelley's Mythmaking* (1959), *The Visionary Company* (1961), *Blake's Apocalypse* (1963), *Yeats* (1970), *A Map of Misreading* (1975), *Kabbalah and Criticism* (1975), *Agon: Toward a Theory of Revisionism* (1982), *The American Religion* (1992), *The Western Canon* (1994), and *Omens of Millennium: The Gnosis of Angels, Dreams, and Resurrection* (1996). *The Anxiety of Influence* (1973) sets forth Professor Bloom's provocative theory of the literary relationships between the great writers and their predecessors. His most recent books include *Shakespeare: The Invention of the Human* (1998), a 1998 National Book Award finalist, *How to Read and Why* (2000), and *Genius: A Mosaic of One Hundred Exemplary Creative Minds* (2002). In 1999, Professor Bloom received the prestigious American Academy of Arts and Letters Gold Medal for Criticism, and in 2002 he received the Catalonia International Prize.

NEIL HEIMS is a freelance writer, editor and researcher. He has a Ph.D in English from the City University of New York.

JENN McKEE is a free-lance writer in Berkley, Michigan. She has earned an MFA in creative writing from Penn State and an MA in English from the University of Georgia, and her fiction has appeared in *Prairie Schooner, Passages North*, and the anthology *Best New American Voices 2003*, edited by Joyce Carol Oates.

PAUL DE MAN was a world-renowned scholar and critic who taught at Bard, Cornell, Johns Hopkins, and Yale. Among his works are *Allegories of Reading: Figural Language in Rousseau, Nietzsche, Rilke, and Proust* (1979), *Blindness and Insight: Essays in the Rhetoric of Contemporary Criticism* (1971), *The Resistance to Theory* (1986), and *The Rhetoric of Romanticism* (1984).

SERGE DOUBROVSKY is Professor of French at New York University. His works include *The Day S.* (1963), *Why New Criticism: Critical and Objectivity* (1966), *A Self-love* (1982), *Autobiographical* (1988), *The Broken Book* (1989), and *Left for Tale* (1999).

S. BEYNON JOHN in addition to writing on both Camus and Sartre, has published articles in *French Studies Bulletin* and *Journal of European Studies*. His book *Anouilh:* L'Alouette *and* Pauvre Bitos was published in 1984.

INDEX